GERMAN GRAMMAR

FOR REVISION AND REFERENCE

By

F. CLARKE, B.Sc.(Econ.)

Senior Modern Language Master,
Scarborough High School

LONDON

G. BELL & SONS, LTD

1945

First published 1936
Reprinted 1940
Reprinted 1945

Printed in Great Britain by
The Camelot Press Ltd., London and Southampton

PREFACE

THIS book is intended as a reference grammar that will be adequate from the beginning of the German course till the student has advanced far enough to consult works like Duden and Muret-Sanders. Possibly its publication may be justified, first, by the increasing amount of time given to German in English secondary schools, and, secondly, by the nature of the text-books now generally used. The modern " course," perhaps written mainly in German and divided into two or more volumes, deals with grammar in its own way, but, after the very elementary stages, it is not adequate as a book of reference.

If pupils are to do accurate work, they must be able to look up quickly and easily any grammatical points that cause difficulty, and it helps both teacher and pupils if they can become familiar with a book of reference by using it for more than one year; I have therefore tried to make the book simple enough for beginners and complete enough for those who have been studying German for three or four years. I have tried to keep specially in mind the needs of School Certificate students, and to emphasise the points on which they commonly go wrong; and the appendix gives suggestions for a weekly revision during the School Certificate year.

The declensions and genders of nouns, which often give a good deal of trouble, are dealt with, I think, rather more fully than is usual, and the lists are arranged in a form that makes them easy to learn by heart. Anyone who takes the trouble to master Chapter III will have little further difficulty with this subject.

Most of the examples are fairly short, and can be easily

remembered; but some questions of style, and of the less common constructions, are illustrated by quotations from German authors. The few biblical quotations are taken from Dr. Hermann Menge's translation. A few of the rules and examples are repeated in different contexts; probably most teachers will not object to a little repetition of this kind. In the declensions, the accusative case is put immediately after the nominative, as many teachers now prefer this order.

The book is based on the usual German authorities, particularly *Der Grosse Duden*. Dr. Otto Basler, of the Deutsche Sprachberatungstelle, Bibliographisches Institut AG. in Leipzig, very kindly allowed me to consult him on several points.

I am deeply indebted to three of my friends for their very helpful advice and criticism. Herr Alfred Wittern, of the Mittelschule, Travemünde, read the MS.; Dr. Herbert Frenzel, of the Dreikönigschule, Dresden, read the proofs; and Mr. G. A. Twentyman, B.A., formerly my colleague and head of the modern side at Manchester Grammar School, read both the MS. and the proofs.

F. C.

SCARBOROUGH, 1936.

CONTENTS

LETTERS, PRONUNCIATION, ETC.

PRONUNCIATION

1. Alphabet.—The following is the German alphabet, with the pronunciation in phonetic script:

		Printed.		*Written.*		
A	a	𝔄	a	*Ol a*		aː
B	b	𝔅	b	*L b*		beː
C	c	ℭ	c	*L c*		tseː
D	d	𝔇	d	*D d*		deː
E	e	𝔈	e	*C e*		eː
F	f	𝔉	f	*F f*		ɛf
G	g	𝔊	g	*G g*		geː
H	h	ℌ	h	*H h*		haː
I	i	ℑ	i	*Y i*		iː
J	j	ℑ	j	*Y j*		jɔt
K	k	𝔎	k	*K k*		kaː
L	l	𝔏	l	*L l*		ɛl
M	m	𝔐	m	*M m*		ɛm
N	n	𝔑	n	*N n*		ɛn
O	o	𝔒	o	*O o*		oː
P	p	𝔓	p	*P p*		peː

	Printed.		Written.		
Q q	𝕼	q			ku:
R r	𝕽	r			ɛr
S s	𝕾	ſ s (final)[1]		(final)[1]	ɛs
T t	𝕿	t			te:
U u	𝖀	u			u
V v	𝖁	v			fau
W w	𝖂	w			ve:
X x	𝖃	x			iks
Y y	𝖄	y			ypsilon
Z z	𝖅	ȝ			tsɛt

2. The vowel sounds are represented in phonetic script as follows:

(a)
a	(1)	a	as in	an	ie	(1)	i:	as in	Lied
	(2)	a:	,,	rasen	o	(1)	ɔ	,,	ob
aa		a:	,,	Aal		(2)	o:	,,	rot
e	(1)	ɛ	,,	fest	oo		o:	,,	Boot
	(2)	e:	,,	her	u	(1)	u	,,	Hund
	(3)	ə	,,	geboten		(2)	u:	,,	Huf
ee		e:	,,	Heer	y	(1)	i	,,	Zylinder
i	(1)	i	,,	in		(2)	y	,,	Daktylus
	(2)	i:	,,	Lid					

(b) Three vowels, **a, o,** and **u,** may undergo modification of sound (Umlaut), and are then written **ä, ö,** and **ü**—spät, schön, früh. These modified vowel sounds used to be indicated by a following **e** (**ae, oe,** and **ue**), and this form is still sometimes used with capital letters—Über (Ueber). In

---

[1] Used only at the end of a word or syllable.

handwriting, the Umlaut is represented by strokes instead of dots.

ä (1) ε as in Hände   ö (1) œ as in zwölf
  (2) ε: ,,   Fähre   (2) ɸ: ,,   stören

ü (1) y as in Glück
  (2) y: ,,   für

(c) Diphthongs:

au au as in aus
äu ɔy ,,   Bäume (the u in au is never modified)
eu ɔy ,,   treu   ei ai as in ein
ai ai ,,   Hain   ey ai ,,   Meyer

3. Consonants. The following are the chief differences between the German and English consonants:

(a) Single consonants:

b, d, and g are pronounced like p, t, and k respectively at the end of a word or syllable, except that the ending =ig is pronounced like ich—abreisen, Handschuh, klug, einig, Einigkeit.

c, which is not often used by itself, is pronounced like ts before e, i, y, or a modified vowel; otherwise it is pronounced like k—circa.

h at the end of a syllable is not pronounced, but makes the preceding vowel long—sehen, lohnen.

j is pronounced like the English y in *young*—jung.

l is pronounced with the tongue against the inside of the front teeth—halten.

r must be rolled. In conversation the uvular r is permissible but not necessary—sehr.

s at the end of a syllable is pronounced like the English *ss*. Before a vowel it is pronounced like the English *z*—Gras, Gräser.

v is pronounced like the English *f*—von.

w is pronounced like the English *v*—wo.

z is pronounced like ts—zu.

(b) Two or more consonants:

ch (1) after a, o, or u is pronounced as in the Scotch *loch* —ach.

(2) After all other letters it is pronounced like the first sound in the English *hue*— idf.

(3) At the beginning of a word it is pronounced as in (2), or like the English *sh* or *k*, according to the derivation of the word—Chemie, Chauſſee, Charakter.

chs is pronounced like *x*, unless the s is a genitive ending or the first letter of a word used in a compound, when the ch and s are pronounced separately—Lachs, (des) Bachs, nachſichtig.

dt is pronounced like t—Stadt.

qu is pronounced like the English *kv*—Quelle.

ſch is pronounced like the English *sh*—ſchaffen.

ſp and ſt at the beginning of a word or syllable are pronounced like the English *shp* and *sht* respectively—Anſpruch, Stadt.

ſſ and ß: ſſ is used only between two vowels the first of which is short; otherwise ß should be used.[1] In fact, ſſ is often written for ß, but this is not strictly correct—müſſen, muß, mußte. Flüſſe (short), Füße (long).

If two s's happen to come together as the last and first letters of words used in compounds, they are not changed to ß—ausſprechen. Both ſſ and ß are pronounced like the English *ss*.

4. The glottal stop is a slight sound, caused by the sudden opening of the glottis, before a vowel at the beginning of a word or syllable. This prevents the liaison that characterises English and French pronunciation. Thus, whereas *an apple* is pronounced without a break, ein Apfel is pronounced as two distinct words.

5. Grimm's Law. The changes of letters between High German and Low German words have been classified by the German philologist Grimm in what is known as Grimm's Law.

(a) The following are examples of the changes of consonants:

b (medial):	haben	lieben	Rabe
v :	have	love	raven

---

[1] In words like flußab, where the ß comes at the end of a part of a compound word, ſſ is not used.

	b (final):	halb	Stab	Weib		
	f :	half	staff	wi*f*e		

pf, f:	Apfel	Pflanze	Pflaume	Haufe	laufen	tief
p :	a*pp*le	*p*lant	*p*lum	hea*p*	lea*p*	dee*p*

d:	das	dick	Distel	drei	durch	Feder
th :	*th*at	*th*ick	*th*istle	*th*ree	*th*rough	fea*th*er

t:	Garten	Saat	Tag	Taube	Teil	trinken
d :	garden	see*d*	*d*ay	*d*ove	*d*eal	*d*rink

s, ss, ß, z:	das	Los	besser	lassen	Hitze	Katze
t :	tha*t*	lo*t*	be*tt*er	le*t*	hea*t*	ca*t*

		zahm	Herz			
		*t*ame	hear*t*			

k:	Kalb	kann	Kuh	Kaufmann	Kerl	Kiste
c, ch :	calf	can	cow	*ch*apman	*ch*url	*ch*est

ch:	brechen	Eiche	Lerche	machen	streichen	suchen
k :	brea*k*	oa*k*	lar*k*	ma*k*e	stro*k*e	see*k*

ch:	doch	durch	fechten	leicht	recht	Sicht
gh :	thou*gh*	throu*gh*	fi*gh*t	li*gh*t	ri*gh*t	si*gh*t

ck:		lecken	stecken	strecken	Brücke	Ecke	Mücke
ck, tch, dg :	lick	stick	stre*tch*	bri*dg*e	e*dg*e	mi*dg*e

g, j:	gestern	Tag	Weg	Jahr	jener	jung
y :	yesterday	day	way	*y*ear	*y*onder	*y*oung

(b) The changes of vowels are much more complicated, and cannot be reduced to any simple general rules. The following examples should not be taken as a general guide to the changes of the vowels in question:

a:	Bart	klar	Waffe	schlafen	Nadel	Straße
ea, ee :	b*ea*rd	cl*ea*r	w*ea*pon	sl*ee*p	n*ee*dle	str*ee*t

ei:	Bein	Geist	Heim	breit	Eiche	Eid
o, oa :	b*o*ne	gh*o*st	h*o*me	br*oa*d	*oa*k	*oa*th

au:	Haus	Maus	sauer	Braue	Sau	Schau
ou, ow :	h*ou*se	m*ou*se	s*ou*r	br*ow*	s*ow*	sh*ow*

u:	Bund	tun	Zunge	Buch	Flut	Stuhl
o, oo :	b*o*nd	d*o*	t*o*ngue	b*oo*k	fl*oo*d	st*oo*l

PUNCTUATION, ETC.

6. Punctuation.

(a) The full stop is used to distinguish ordinal from cardinal numbers: Am 15. Januar, *On the 15th January.*

(b) The exclamation mark is used more freely in German than in English. It is often used in heading notices: Vorsicht! *Caution.* It is used in beginning letters: Sehr geehrter Herr! *Dear Sir.* It is also used after the imperative when the English would generally use a full stop: Kommen Sie bald wieder! *Come again soon.*

(c) The colon and semicolon are used much as in English. A colon is used in preference to a comma when beginning a quotation: Da lachte sie hell auf und sagte: „Das ist gut; das mag ich alles sehr gern leiden."

(d) The comma is dealt with under the various parts of speech; see index.

7. The apostrophe.

(a) For the use of the apostrophe after proper names ending in a sibilant, see paragraph **48** (c).

(b) Letters omitted are represented by an apostrophe (as in English, e.g., *How's that?*): Wie geht's? *How are you?*

(c) If such a contraction forms a recognised word, no apostrophe is used: aufs for auf das; andre for andere.

8. The hyphen.

(a) A hyphen is sometimes used after proper names used as adjectives: das Bismarckdenkmal or das Bismarck=Denkmal, *the Bismarck Monument.* Names of streets are generally spelt without hyphens, unless they contain a Christian name die Hindenburgstraße; die Adolf=Hitler=Straße.

(b) A hyphen is sometimes used to join long words; there is no hard and fast rule: die Wirtschafts=Beilage, *economic supplement*; der Leichtathletik=Länderkampf, *international athletic contest.*

(c) A hyphen is used to avoid repeating part of a compound word: die Sommer= und Winterferien (instead of die Sommer=ferien und Winterferien); die Waldblumen und =Pflanzen (instead of die Waldblumen und Waldpflanzen).

9. Separation of Syllables.

(a) If a compound word has to be divided, it is divided into separate words: der Vor=an=schlag; das Haus=tier; das Rat=haus. Divisions inside a single word are made as follows:

(b) If two vowels are separated by a consonant, the hyphen precedes the consonant: Die Stu=dien; die Bie=nen.

(c) The letters ch, ph, th, sch, and ß, which form single sounds, are not separated. The letters ss may be separated: das Was=ser. The letters ck, if separated, are written k=k: die Flok=ken.

(d) The letters st are not separated: der Mei=ster.

(e) Otherwise, if two or more consonants come together, the hyphen is put before the last: der Fun=ke; kämp=fen.

10. Emphasis.

The usual way of emphasising a word in German is to print it in specially spaced type [see also ein and e i n, paragraph **178** (c)]: Im Jahre 1934 sind in Amerika 36 000 P e r s o n e n d u r c h A u t o s g e t ö t e t worden.

CAPITAL LETTERS

11. Capital letters are used in German:

(a) For nouns: das Buch, *the book*.

(b) For other parts of speech used as nouns; particularly:

(i) Gerunds: das Reisen, *travelling*.

(ii) Adjectives and participles used as nouns: der (die) Blinde, *the blind (wo)man*; der (die) Angeklagte, *the accused*.

(iii) Adjectives after etwas, nichts, etc. [see paragraph **52** (b)]: etwas Großes, *something big*.

(iv) Indefinite neuter adjectives after das: das Beste, *the best thing*.

(c) For adjectives and numerals used in names or titles: Friedrich der Große, *Frederick the Great*; die Britischen Inseln, *the British Isles*.

(d) For adjectives formed by adding =er to the names of towns: die Berliner Läden, *the shops of Berlin*.

(e) For the pronouns du and ihr (when used in correspondence) and Sie meaning *you*; and also for their corresponding possessive adjectives, dein and euer (in correspondence) and Jhr.

12. Small letters are used:

(a) For pronouns, numerals, and adjectives referring to a particular person or thing: jemand, *someone*; der erste, der zweite, der älteste (dieser Jungen), *the first, the second, the eldest (of these boys)*.

(b) In superlative adverb phrases: am besten; aufs beste.

(c) For adjectives used after prepositions: im allgemeinen, *in general*; über kurz oder lang, *sooner or later*; bei weitem, *by far*.

(d) For nouns used in a special relation to a particular verb, being sometimes treated as separable prefixes: schuld sein, *to be at fault*; weh tun, *to hurt*; teilnehmen, *to take part*; achtgeben, *to pay attention*.

ABBREVIATIONS

13. Abbreviations. The following abbreviations are common:

a., auch	Ew., Euer, Eure
a.D., außer Dienst	Ez., Einzahl
A.G., Aktiengesellschaft	ff., folgende (Seiten)
ahd., althochdeutsch	Fr., Frau
Anm., Anmerkung	Frl., Fräulein
Bd., Band	geb. (or *), geboren
bzw., beziehungsweise	geb., gebunden
d.h., das heißt	Gebr., Gebrüder
d.J., dieses Jahres	gef., gefälligst
d.M., dieses Monats	gest. (or †), gestorben
E.V., Eingetragener Verein	G.m.b.H., Gesellschaft mit be-
evtl., eventuell	schränkter Haftung

ha, Hektar
i.R., im Ruhestand(e)
kg, Kilogramm
Kgl., Königlich
km, Kilometer
m, Meter
M, Mark
mhd., mittelhochdeutsch
Mz., Mehrzahl
N(a)chf., Nachfolger
n. Chr., nach Christus
nhd., neuhochdeutsch
n.J., nächsten Jahres
n.M., nächsten Monats
NO, Nordost
Nr., Nummer
NS., Nachschrift
NW, Nordwest
od., oder
Pf., Pfennig
PS, Pferdestärke
qm, Quadratmeter
RM, Reichsmark
s., sieh(e)
S., Seite
S.M., Seine Majestät

s.o., siehe oben
SO, Südost
sog., sogenannt
s.u., siehe unten
SW, Südwest
u., und
u.a., und andere(s); unter an-
    derm; unter andern
u.ä., und ähnliche(s)
u.a.m., und andere(s) mehr
U.A.w.g., Um Antwort wird
    gebeten
u.dgl.(m.), und dergleichen (mehr)
usf., und so fort
usw., und so weiter
v., von
v. Chr., vor Christus
vgl., vergleiche
v.H., vom Hundert
v.J., vorigen Jahres
v.M., vorigen Monats
W.! Wenden!
Wwe., Witwe
z.B., zum Beispiel
z.Z., zur Zeit

II

THE ARTICLES

THE DEFINITE ARTICLE

14. The definite article.

	Masculine	*Feminine*	*Neuter*	*Plural*	
N.	der	die	das	die	the
A.	den	die	das	die	the
G.	des	der	des	der	of the
D.	dem	der	dem	den	to the

15. Contraction of the definite article with prepositions. Der, das, and dem, when not emphasised, are often contracted with certain prepositions as follows:

an das, ans	in das, ins
an dem, am	in dem, im
auf das, aufs	um das, ums
bei dem, beim	von dem, vom
durch das, durchs	zu der, zur
für das, fürs	zu dem, zum

Similar contractions are less often made with hinter, über, unter, and vor.

16. Use of the definite article. The definite article is used in German:

(a) With abstract nouns:

Die Zeit arbeitet für uns   Time is on our side.

(b) Sometimes with concrete nouns when it is not used in English:[1]

Der Mensch ist sterblich	Man is mortal
Beim Frühstück, Mittagessen usw.	At breakfast, lunch, etc.
Mit dem Zug (Dampfer)	By train (steamer)
In die Kirche, in die Schule, in die Stadt gehen	To go to church, to school, to town

(c) With the names of days, months, and seasons:

Am Montag, im Juni, im Herbst	On Monday, in June, in autumn

(d) With masculine and feminine names of countries,[2] geographical features generally, and streets:

Die Schweiz, die Themse, die Hindenburgstraße	Switzerland, the Thames, Hindenburg Street

(e) With proper names preceded by an adjective:

Das heutige Deutschland	Present-day Germany
Der junge Georg	Young George

(f) With unqualified names of persons, (i) to express familiarity, which may imply affection or contempt; or (ii) to show the case [see paragraph **48 (d)**] :

Sie kamen nie alleine, der Zieten und der Fritz[3]	They never came alone, Zieten and Fred

---

[1] On the other hand, the names of substances are generally used without the article, as in English: Eisen ist hart, *Iron is hard*; Wasser ist uns nötig, *Water is necessary for us.* See also paragraph **17 (b)**.

[2] All names of towns, and most names of countries, are neuter, and do not take the article when used alone: Wien, *Vienna*; Österreich, *Austria*.

[3] Referring to General von Zieten and Frederick the Great

(g) Often instead of possessive adjectives, especially when referring to clothes or parts of the body [see also paragraph 449 (c) on the dative of interest or advantage]:

Er hat (sich) den Arm gebrochen	He has broken his arm
Beide schüttelten den Kopf	They both shook their heads
Er stieß ihn an den Arm	He knocked his (*i.e.*, some-one else's) arm
Er stieß sich an den Arm	He knocked his (own) arm

(h) With infinitives used as nouns, and with nouns ending in =ung similarly used:

Im Vorbeigehen	In passing
Bei der Untersuchung der Sache	When the matter was (or is) investigated

(i) Distributively, where the English indefinite article is used:

Zwei Mark das Pfund	Two shillings a pound
Zweimal in der Woche, im Monat, im Jahre	Twice a week, a month, a year

17. The definite article is not used:

(a) Generally when two or more nouns are closely joined in one idea:

Stadt und Land, Wind und Wetter, Hand in Hand	Town and country, wind and weather, hand in hand

(b) Often after prepositions:

Zu Fuß, bei Tisch, nach Norden	On foot, at table, northwards

(c) Often in proverbs:

Furcht in Gefahr ist Schwäche	Fear in danger is weakness
Jugend vergeht, Tugend besteht	Youth passes, virtue lasts

(d) After an inflected form of all [see paragraph 126 (b)]:

Alle Jungen sind fort	All the boys have gone

(e) In certain other expressions; *e.g.*:

Rat halten	To take counsel
Eile haben	To be in a hurry
Ein Brief folgenden Inhalts	A letter reading as follows

THE INDEFINITE ARTICLE

18. The indefinite article.

	Masculine	Feminine	Neuter	
N.	ein	eine	ein	a(n)
A.	einen	eine	ein	a(n)
G.	eines	einer	eines	of a(n)
D.	einem	einer	einem	to a(n)

19. The indefinite article is not used:

(a) Before a noun used without an adjective after sein or werden, if rank or occupation is denoted:

Er ist Lehrer geworden	He has become a school-master
Er ist Mitglied des Unterhauses	He is a member of the House of Commons

(b) Before a noun in apposition after als:

Er sprach als Freund	He spoke as a friend

(c) Often after prepositions; in some phrases the definite article is used instead:

Ein Land ohne König	A country without a king
Mit schwerem Herzen	With a heavy heart
Mit lauter Stimme	In a loud voice
Zum Spaß	For a joke
Im Nu	In an instant

(d) When translating *not a*. Generally, nicht ein means *not one*, and *not a* is kein:

Das ist kein Fehler	That is not a mistake

20. 'Some' or 'any' generally need not be translated before a noun, though ein bißchen, etwas, or ein wenig are sometimes used in the singular, and einige or ein paar in the plural:

Haben Sie Kaffee getrunken?	Have you had any coffee?
Es liegen (einige or ein paar) Briefe auf dem Tisch)	There are some letters on the table

21. Repetition of the article.

(a) The article must be repeated before a second noun if a different form is needed, or if the case or number is different:

Der Bruder und die Schwester meines Freundes	My friend's brother and sister
Die Dame und die Kinder	The lady and children

(b) When the form, case, and number are the same, the article is not repeated if the two nouns are thought of as a collective whole:

In den Städten und Dörfern unsres Landes sind viele alte Gebäude	In the towns and villages of our country there are many old buildings.
Die Städte und die Dörfer unsres Landes haben nicht dieselbe Regierungsform	The towns and the villages of our country have not the same form of government

III

NOUNS

THE DECLENSIONS

22. The declensions.

(a) German nouns are classified into three declensions, strong, weak, and mixed.

(b) All feminine nouns remain unchanged in the singular.

(c) Strong nouns, if masculine or neuter, add *-es* or *-s* in the genitive singular.[1]   The formation of the plural divides all strong nouns into three main classes; *i.e.*, those

(i) Unchanged, but with the stem vowel **a, o,** or **u** sometimes modified.

(ii) Adding *-e*, with the stem vowel **a, o,** or **u** generally modified.

(iii) Adding *-er*, with the stem vowel **a, o,** or **u** always modified.

(d) Weak nouns add *-en* or *-n* in all cases, masculines in the singular and plural, and feminines only in the plural.

(e) Nouns of the mixed declensions are strong in the singular and weak in the plural.

(f) Classes 2 and 3 of the strong declension add *-es* in the genitive singular and *-e* in the dative singular.   This *-e* is often dropped in both cases, but there is no definite rule about it—it depends on how it sounds to the speaker.

Nouns ending in a sibilant must keep the *-e* in the genitive, and monosyllables with a long vowel and ending in a consonant generally do so: das Glas, des Glases, *glass*; der Sohn, des Sohnes, *son*.

(g) In the plural of all nouns the genitive and accusative are like the nominative, and the dative ends in *-en* or *-n*.

[1] Except for the small group given in paragraph **23 (c)**.

23. Strong declension, class 1.

(a) Model A: der Onkel, *uncle.*

	Singular	*Plural*
N.	der Onkel	die Onkel
A.	den Onkel	die Onkel
G.	des Onkels	der Onkel
D.	dem Onkel	den Onkeln

Nouns ending in *en do not take an extra *n in the dative plural.

To model A belong:

(i) Most masculines and neuters ending in *el, *en, and *er.

Most nouns with these endings are masculine, some are neuter [see paragraphs **38, 39,** and **40**], and some in *el and *er are feminine [see paragraphs **36** and **37**].

The following is a list of some of the masculines in common use. Besides these, there are many masculines formed by adding *er to the stems of verbs; *e.g.,* der Diener, *servant;* der Führer, *leader;* der Leser, *reader.*

Engel, angel	Gipfel, summit	Deckel, lid
Enkel, grandson	Gürtel, belt	Löffel, spoon
Esel, donkey	Himmel, sky	Nebel, fog
Flügel, wing	Hügel, hill	Kessel, kettle
Schlüssel, key	Ärmel, sleeve	Tempel, temple
Stengel, stalk	Zettel, label	Teufel, devil
Stiefel, boot	Zweifel, doubt	Titel, title
Sessel, arm-chair	Adel, nobility	Tadel, blame
Balken, beam	Bogen,[1] bow	Rahmen, frame
Besen, broom	Felsen, rock	Rasen, turf
Brunnen, well	Knochen, bone	Rücken, back
Braten, roast meat	Spaten, spade	Regen, rain

[1] Plural sometimes die Bögen.

Schatten, shade
Schinken, ham
Schlitten, sledge
Segen, blessing

Haken, hook
Husten, cough
Kuchen, cake
Reifen, tyre

Wagen, carriage
Weizen, wheat
Schnupfen, cold in
  the head
Streif(en), strip

Nord(en), north
Süd(en), south
Ost(en), east
West(en), west

Bettler, beggar
Bürger, citizen
Jäger, hunter
Ritter, knight

Gegner, opponent
Gletscher, glacier
Schneider, tailor
Schnitter, reaper

Koffer, trunk
Körper, body
Kellner, waiter
Keller, cellar

Adler, eagle
Eimer, pail
Meister, master
Teller, plate

Pfarrer, parson
Puder, powder
Fehler, mistake
Flieger, airman

Schäfer, shepherd
Schaffner, conductor
Schalter, booking-office
Tiger, tiger

(ii) All nouns ending in **-chen** and **-lein**; *e.g.*, das Mädchen, *girl*; das Fräulein, *young lady.* See paragraph **55.**

(iii) Neuters beginning with **Ge-** and ending in **-e**; *e.g.*, das Gebirge, *range of mountains.*

(b) Model B: der Nagel, *nail.*

Singular	*Plural*
N. der Nagel	die Nägel
A. den Nagel	die Nägel
G. des Nagels	der Nägel
D. dem Nagel	den Nägeln

Nouns ending in **-en** do not take an extra **-n** in the dative plural.

To model B belong:

(i) Die Mutter, *mother,* and die Tochter, *daughter* (which, being feminine, do not change in the singular), and das Kloster, *convent.*

(ii) The following masculines:

Acker, field	Hafen, harbour
Apfel, apple	Hammer, hammer
Garten, garden	Mangel, want
Graben, ditch	Mantel, cloak
Faden, thread	Laden, shop
Nagel, nail	Vater, father
Sattel, saddle	Bruder, brother
Schnabel, beak	Ofen, stove
Schwager, brother-in-law	Vogel, bird
Schaden, damage	Boden, ground

Käse, cheese

(c) Model C: der Name, *name*.

	Singular	Plural
N.	der Name	die Namen
A.	den Namen	die Namen
G.	des Namens	der Namen
D.	dem Namen	den Namen

Here the ⸗n of the nominative singular is missing; otherwise it is like model A. The following nouns belong to it:

(i) Das Herz, *heart* (which does not change in the accusative singular).

(ii) The following masculines:

Friede, peace	Buchstabe, letter of the alphabet
Glaube, faith	Gedanke, thought
Haufe, heap	Wille, will
Name, name	Same, seed

24. Strong declension, class 2.

(a) Model A: der Sohn, *son*.

	Singular	Plural
N.	der Sohn	die Söhne
A.	den Sohn	die Söhne
G.	des Sohnes	der Söhne
D.	dem Sohne	den Söhnen

Nouns with a double vowel in this group drop one of them in the plural: der Saal, die Säle, *hall*.

To model A belong:

(i) Most masculine monosyllables and their compounds. This group therefore contains a very large number of nouns in common use; *e.g.*, der Arzt, *doctor*; der Fluß, *river*; der Pflug, *plough*; der Rock, *coat*; der Stuhl, *chair*; der Wolf, *wolf*.

(ii) The following masculines of more than one syllable:

Altar, altar	Herzog,[2] duke
Anlaß, cause	Marschall, marshal
Vertrag,[1] treaty	Palast, palace
Einwand, objection	Choral, anthem
Vorwand, pretext	Kanal, channel
Genuß, enjoyment	Admiral, admiral
Gesang, hymn	General, general
Bischof, bishop	Kardinal, cardinal

(iii) Das Floß, *raft*.

(b) Model B: das Jahr, *year*.

	Singular	Plural
N.	das Jahr	die Jahre
A.	das Jahr	die Jahre
G.	des Jahres	der Jahre
D.	dem Jahre	den Jahren

To model B belong:

(i) Most neuters, except those ending in =chen, =lein, =e, =el, =en, =er, =tum, and =um, and those given in paragraph 25.

The following list contains the commonest neuter monosyllables, and a few other nouns with various endings, belonging to this group:

Blech, metal plate	Ding,[3] thing	Fell, skin
Blei, lead	Eis, ice	Fest, festival
Blut, blood	Erz, ore	Fleisch, meat
Boot, boat	Brot, bread	Maß, measure

---

[1] And other compounds of =trag.   [2] Plural sometimes die Herzoge.
[3] Plural sometimes die Dinger (used disparagingly).

Gift, poison
Glück, fortune
Gold, gold
Gas, gas

Haar, hair
Laub, foliage
Lob, praise
Los, lot

Heer, army
Meer, sea
Öl, oil
Seil, rope

Roß, horse
Salz, salt
Stroh, straw
Bein, leg

Heft, handle
Kinn, chin
Kreuz, cross
Knie, knee

Mahl, meal
Mal, time
Mehl, flour
Moos, moss

Pferd, horse
Pfund, pound
Pult, desk
Riff, reef

Schaf, sheep
Schilf, reed
Stück, piece
Schwein, pig
Rohr, tube
Zelt, tent
Zeug, stuff
Ziel, aim

Heu, hay
Heil, welfare
Heim, home
Vieh, cattle

Jahr, year
Paar, pair
Obst, fruit
Beil, hatchet

Reh, deer
Recht, right
Reich, realm
Schiff, ship

Netz, net
Werk, work
Wrack, wreck
Spiel, game

Alphabet, alphabet
Billett, ticket
Defizit, deficit
Diplom, diploma
Dutzend, dozen
Edikt, edict
Erbteil, inheritance
Gegenteil, contrast
Urteil,[1] judgment
Elend, misery
Honorar, fee
Institut, institute
Kabinett, cabinet
Klima,[2] climate

Konzert, concert
Labyrinth, labyrinth
Manuskript, manuscript
Monopol, monopoly
Organ,[3] organ
Paket, parcel
Patent, patent
Problem, problem
Programm, programme
Prozent, percentage
System, system
Talent, talent
Telegramm, telegram
Telephon, telephone

Verbot, prohibition

[1] The other compounds of der Teil are masculine, but der or das Abteil, *compartment*, may be masculine or neuter.

[2] Plural, die Klimate.

[3] Not the musical instrument, which is die Orgel.

(ii) Nouns ending in =nis, whether feminine or neuter; *e.g.*, die Beſorgnis, *care*; das Bildnis, *portrait*. The =s is doubled before e, and the feminine nouns do not change in the singular. The genitive singular is therefore der Beſorgnis and des Bildniſſes, and the nominative plural is die Beſorgniſſe and die Bildniſſe.

(iii) Most masculines of more than one syllable, except (1) compounds of a noun that modifies in the plural (*e.g.*, der Entſchluß, *resolution*) and (2) those ending in =e, =el, =en, and =er.

(iv) The following masculine monosyllables, besides many others in less common use:

Aal, eel	Druck, print	Dolch, dagger
Akt, act	Halm, stalk	Dom, cathedral
Arm, arm	Hauch, breath	Forſt, forest
Ruf, call	Huf, hoof	Hund, dog
Grat, ridge	Laut, sound	Pol, pole
Kork, cork	Mond, moon	Puls, pulse
Kurs, course	Ort, place	Punkt, point
Mund,[1] mouth	Grad, degree	Pfad, path

Sproß, sprout	Schuft, rascal
Stoff, stuff	Schuh, shoe
Tag, day	Schmuck, finery
Thron, throne	Mohn, poppy

c) Model C: die Hand, *hand*.

Singular	Plural
N. die Hand	die Hände
A. die Hand	die Hände
G. der Hand	der Hände
D. der Hand	den Händen

To model C belong the following feminines:

Angſt, anxiety	Bank, bench	Kraft, strength
Axt, axe	Braut, bride	Kuh, cow
Bruſt, breast	Luſt, pleasure	Kunſt, art
Gruft, tomb	Luft, air	Kluft, cleft

[1] Plural sometimes die Münder.

Gans, goose	Zunft, guild	Schnur, string
Maus, mouse	Not, need	Stadt, town
Magd, maid	Nuß, nut	Haut, skin
Macht, power	Nacht, night	Hand, hand
	Faust, fist	
	Frucht, fruit	
	Wurst, sausage	
	Wand, wall	

25. Strong declension, class 3.

Model: das Dorf, *village.*

Singular	*Plural*
N. das Dorf	die Dörfer
A. das Dorf	die Dörfer
G. des Dorfes	der Dörfer
D. dem Dorfe	den Dörfern

To this class belong:

(i) Nouns ending in **-tum**; *e.g.,* der Irrtum, *error;* das Herzogtum, *duchy.*

(ii) The following masculines:

Gott, God	Rand, edge
Geist, spirit	Strauch, shrub
Mann,[1] man	Wald, wood
Leib, body	Wurm, worm

(iii) The following neuters:

Amt, office	Blatt, leaf	Ei, egg
Bad, bath	Brett, plank	Huhn, hen
Bild, picture	Buch, book	Faß, cask
Dach, roof	Fach, compartment	Feld, field
Dorf, village	Haupt, head	Kalb, calf
Grab, grave	Haus, house	Kind, child
Gut, estate	Holz, wood	Kleid, dress
Geld, money	Horn, horn	Korn, grain

[1] Compound nouns ending in -mann usually form their plural in -leute, *e.g.,* der Kaufmann, die Kaufleute, *tradesman, tradespeople.*

Kraut, herb	Maul,[1] mouth	Rad, wheel
Lamm, lamb	Nest, nest	Reis, twig
Loch, hole	Pfand, pledge	Rind, ox
Glas, glass	Gras, grass	Glied, limb
Schild, signboard	Tal, valley	Gehalt, salary
Schloß, castle	Volk, people	Gemach, apartment
Schwert, sword	Weib, woman	Gemüt, mind
Lid, eyelid	Lied, song	Geschlecht, race, sex
		Gespenst, ghost
		Gewand, garment

26. Weak declension.

(a) Model A: der Knabe, *boy.*

	Singular	Plural
N.	der Knabe	die Knaben
A.	den Knaben	die Knaben
G.	des Knaben	der Knaben
D.	dem Knaben	den Knaben

If the noun ends in =e, =el, or =er, only =n is added to the stem; otherwise =en is added.

To model A belong:

(i) Most masculines ending in =e. [The exceptions are der Käse, *cheese,* in paragraph **23** (b) and the few nouns in paragraph **23** (c).] This group contains a number of nouns denoting living beings; *e.g.,* der Affe, *monkey;* der Bote, messenger; der Franzose, *Frenchman;* der Junge, *boy;* der Löwe, *lion;* der Matrose, *sailor;* der Neffe, *nephew.*

(ii) Some masculines of foreign origin, mostly denoting persons. Common endings are =at, =ant, =ent, and ist; *e.g.:*

Soldat, soldier	Barbar, barbarian
Elefant, elephant	Kamerad, comrade
Kommandant, commander	Monarch, monarch
Präsident, president	Philosoph, philosopher
Student, student	Photograph, photographer
Dentist, dentist	Poet, poet

---

[1] Of animals.

(iii) The following masculines:

Ahn,[1] ancestor	Fürst, prince	Funke, spark
Bauer,[1] peasant	Prinz, prince	Geck, fop [being
Bursch, lad	Graf, count	Mensch, human
Bär, bear	Herr,[2] gentleman	Narr, buffoon

Held, hero	Christ, Christian
Hirt, shepherd	Oberst, colonel
Spatz, sparrow	Ochs, ox
Vorfahr, ancestor	Tor, fool

(b) Model B: die Blume, *flower*.

	Singular	*Plural*
N.	die Blume	die Blumen
A.	die Blume	die Blumen
G.	der Blume	der Blumen
D.	der Blume	den Blumen

To this model belong most feminines. [For an important list of exceptions, see paragraph **24** (c).] Those ending in =in (*e.g.*, die Lehrerin, *schoolmistress*) have the plural =innen.

The great majority of nouns ending in =e are feminine, and belong to this group; *e.g.*, die Ecke, *corner*; die Farbe, *colour*; die Lerche, *lark*; die Straße, *street*; die Welle, *wave*; die Wolke, *cloud*.

The following list contains the commonest feminine monosyllables, and a few other nouns with various endings, belonging to this group:

Art, kind	Bahn, path	Fahrt, journey
Bö, gust	Bai, bay	Furt, ford
Wahl, choice	Burg, castle	Frau, woman
Wut, rage	Brut, brood	Flut, flood

---

[1] Sometimes declined as in paragraph **27** (mixed declension).
[2] Changes into Herrn in the singular and Herren in the plural.

Form, form
Frist, space of time
Front, front
Glut, glow

Haft, arrest
Jagd, chase
List, cunning
Saat, seed

Schar, flock
Schmach, disgrace
Schuld, debt
Uhr, clock

Acht, care
Fracht, freight
Pacht, lease
Gicht, gout

Gunst, favour
Huld, grace
Kur, cure
Kost, food

Milch, milk
Pest, pestilence
Pein, pain
Tat, deed

Schrift, writing
Tür, door
Welt, world
Qual, torture

Pracht, pomp
Schlacht, battle
Tracht, costume
Pflicht, duty

Sucht, disease
Wucht, weight
Zucht, breeding
Sicht, sight

Hast, haste
Rast, rest
Last, burden
Post, post

Scham, shame
Schau, show
Scheu, shyness
Spur, trace

Stirn, forehead
Zeit, time
Zier, ornament
Zahl, number

Bucht, bay
Flucht, flight
Schlucht, gorge
Schicht, layer

Anmut, grace
Armut, poverty
Demut, humility
Großmut, magnanimity
Langmut, patience
Sanftmut, gentleness
Wehmut,[1] melancholy

Ausfuhr, export
Einfuhr, import

Rückkehr, return[2]

Anstalt, establishment

Antwort, answer

Arbeit, work

Einfalt, simplicity

Firma, firm

Gegend, district

Gegenwart, presence

Jugend, youth

Tugend, virtue

Mitgift, dowry

Predigt, sermon

Vernunft, reason

[1] The other compounds of der Mut are masculine.
[2] The other compounds of -kehr are feminine, except der Verkehr, traffic.

27. Mixed declension.

Model: der Staat, *state.*

Singular	*Plural*
N. der Staat	die Staaten
A. den Staat	die Staaten
G. des Staates	der Staaten
D. dem Staate	den Staaten

To this declension belong:

(i) Some nouns of foreign origin, the most important of which are those ending in =or—*e.g.*, der Doktor, *doctor*—and those ending in =um, which form the plural by changing =um into =en; *e.g.*, das Studium, *study.*

(ii) The following masculines:

Nerv, nerve	Staat, state	Lorbeer,[2] laurel
Psalm, psalm	Stachel, sting	Nachbar,[3] neighbour
Schmerz, pain	Strahl, ray	Papagei, parrot
Dorn, thorn	Sporn,[1] spur	Untertan, subject
		Vetter, cousin
		Gevatter, godfather, old friend

(iii) The following neuters:

Auge, eye	Bett, bed	Insekt, insect
Ende, end	Hemd, shirt	Interesse, interest
Ohr, ear	Leid, sorrow	Statut, statute

28. The following nouns have two plurals with different meanings:

das Band	die Bänder, ribbons	die Bande, ties (bonds)
die Bank	die Bänke, benches	die Banken, banks (money)
das Gesicht	die Gesichter, faces	die Gesichte, visions
der Laden	die Läden, shops	die Laden, shutters
das Land	die Länder, separate countries	die Lande, countries collectively

---

[1] Plural, die Sporen.   [2] Plural, die Lorbeeren.
[3] Plural, die Nachbarn.

das Licht	die Lichter, lights	die Lichte, candles
der Strauß	die Sträuße, bouquets	die Strauße, ostriches
das Tuch	die Tücher, shawls	die Tuche, cloths
das Wort	die Wörter, single words	die Worte, sentences

29. Nouns taking -s in the plural. In popular speech, the forms die Jungens, die Kerls, and die Mädels are often used for the plural of der Junge, *boy*; der Kerl, *fellow*; and das Mädel, *girl*.

30. Foreign nouns.

(a) Some nouns of foreign origin that are used in German have not been incorporated into any of the ordinary declensions. Such are das Auto, *motor-car*; der Bankier, *banker*; das Hotel, *hotel*; der Klub, *club*. They are declined as follows:

Singular	*Plural*
N. das Auto	die Autos
A. das Auto	die Autos
G. des Autos	der Autos
D. dem Auto	den Autos

(b) A few are feminine; *e.g.*, die Kamera, *camera*. These are declined in the same way, except that they do not change in the singular.

(c) Some may be treated as foreign words, taking -s in the plural, or as German words, forming the plural according to the ordinary declensions. Such are der Lift, *lift*; der Park, *park*; der Start, *start*; der Streik, *strike*; der Tunnel, *tunnel*.

31. Names of days and months.

(a) The -s in the genitive singular is sometimes omitted:

Das Konzert des vorigen Donnerstag(s)	Last Thursday's concert
Die Schönheit des Mai(s)	The beauty of May

3

(b) The genitive is not generally used after der **Anfang,** *beginning;* die **Mitte,** *middle;* and das **Ende,** *end:*

Er reiſte Anfang Januar, (Mitte Februar, gegen Ende März) ab	He left at the beginning of January (in the middle of February, towards the end of March)

THE GENDERS

32. The genders. The gender of most German nouns cannot be told from the meaning or from the ending; and the best way is to learn every noun with the definite article, **der, die,** or **das.** The following rules are useful as far as they go:

33. Masculines:

(a) Names of seasons, months, and days:

Der **Frühling, Sommer, Herbſt, Winter;** *spring, summer,* etc.

Der **Januar (Hartung), Februar (Hornung), März (Lenzing), April (Oſtermond), Mai (Wonnemond), Juni (Brachmond), Juli (Heuert), Auguſt (Ernting), September (Scheiding), Oktober (Gilbhart), November (Neblung), Dezember (Julmond);** *January, February,* etc.

Der **Sonntag, Montag, Dienstag, Mittwoch, Donnerstag, Freitag, Sonnabend** or **Samstag**[1]; *Sunday, Monday,* etc.

(b) Most nouns ending in **=ich, =ig, =ling, =el, =en** (except infinitives), and **=er;** *e.g.,* der **Teppich,** *carpet;* der **Honig,** *honey;* der **Lehrling,** *apprentice;* der **Vogel,** *bird;* der **Hafen,** *harbour;* der **Fehler,** *fault.* [See lists in paragraph **23 (a).**]

(c) Most nouns that form the stems of verbs; *e.g.,* der **Rat,** *advice.*

34. Feminines:

(a) Most nouns ending in **=e** and not beginning with **Ge=,** not denoting male beings; *e.g.,* die **Rache,** *revenge.*

---

[1] Used mainly in South Germany.

(b) Most nouns ending in **-cht** and not beginning with **Ge-**; *e.g.*, die Nacht, *night*.

(c) Nouns ending in **-ei, -heit, -keit, -in, -schaft**, and **-ung**; *e.g.*, die Bäckerei, *bakery*; die Echtheit, *genuineness*; die Heiterkeit, *cheerfulness*; die Königin, *queen*; die Freundschaft, *friendship*; die Haltung, *attitude*.

(d) Nouns of foreign origin ending in **-nz, -ie, -ik, -ion, -tät**, and **-ur**; *e.g.*, die Existenz, *existence*; die Harmonie, *harmony*; die Musik, *music*; die Mission, *mission*; die Universität, *university*; die Kreatur, *creature*.

35. Neuters:

(a) Infinitives used as nouns; *e.g.*, das Rechnen, *calculating, arithmetic*.

(b) All names of towns and most names of countries (exceptions: die Schweiz, *Switzerland*; die Türkei, *Turkey*): Köln, *Cologne*; Pommern, *Pomerania*.

(c) All nouns ending in **-chen, -lein, -ment, -sal**, and **-um**, and most of those ending in **-al, -at, -ier, -nis, -sel**, and **-tum**; *e.g.*, das Mädchen, *girl*; das Fräulein, *young lady*; das Element, *element*; das Scheusal, *monster*; das Studium, *study*; das Ideal, *ideal*; das Attentat, *outrage*; das Klavier, *piano*; das Verhältnis, *proportion*; das Rätsel, *riddle*; das Herzogtum, *duchy*.

(d) Most nouns beginning with **Ge-**; *e.g.*, das Gebäude, *building*.

36. Feminines ending in **-el**.

Achsel, shoulder	Eichel, acorn	Fackel, torch
Amsel, blackbird	Insel, island	Fiedel, fiddle
Angel, hinge	Orgel, organ	Formel, formula
Bibel, Bible	Fibel, primer	Fabel, fable
Dattel, date (fruit)	Geißel, scourge	Regel, rule
Deichsel, shaft	Kanzel, pulpit	Wurzel, root
Drossel, thrush	Pappel, poplar	Nadel, needle
Gabel, fork	Fessel, fetter	Nessel, nettle

Klausel, clause   Semmel, roll   Schachtel, box
Klingel, small bell   Sichel, sickle   Schaufel, shovel
Kugel, ball   Staffel, step, rung   Mandel, almond
Koppel, couple   Stoppel, stubble   Mistel, mistletoe

Schaukel, swing   Schüssel, dish
Tafel, table, board   Zwiebel, onion
Trommel, drum   and
Distel, thistle   Kartoffel, potato

37. Feminines ending in =er.

Ader, vein   Jungfer, spinster   Faser, fibre
Ammer, yellow-   Schwester, sister   Feder, feather
    hammer   Tochter, daughter   Fiber, fibre
Auster, oyster   Mutter, mother   Feier, holiday
Butter, butter

Folter, torment   Kammer, room   Oper, opera
Leber, liver   Klammer, clamp   Order, order
Lauer, ambush   Marter, torture   Schulter, shoulder
Leier, lyre   Mauer, wall   Dauer, duration

Nummer, number
Ziffer, figure
Wimper, eyelash
Trauer, grief

38. Neuters ending in =el.

Bündel, bundle   Möbel,[1] furniture   Rudel, herd
Übel, evil   Segel, sail   Dunkel, darkness
Kabel, cable   Siegel, seal   Exempel, example
Mittel, means   Drittel,[2] third   Kapitel, chapter

39. Neuters ending in =en.

Almosen, alms   Fohlen, foal   Laken, sheet
Becken, basin   Kissen, cushion   Lehen, fief
Eisen, iron   Wappen, coat-of-   Leinen, linen
Omen, omen   arms   Examen, examina-
    Zeichen, sign   tion

[1] Generally used in the plural.
[2] Similarly das Viertel, *quarter*; das Fünftel, *fifth part*, etc.

40. Neuters ending in =er.

Alter, age	Banner, banner	Gitter, trellis
Ufer, shore	Fenster, window	Gatter, railing
Abenteuer, adventure	Futter, fodder	Opfer, sacrifice
	Feuer, fire	Fieber, fever
Kloster, convent	Leder, leather	Messer, knife
Kupfer, copper	Liter,[1] litre	Meter,[1] metre
and	Lager, couch	Muster, model
Kaliber, calibre	Luder, carrion	Fuder, cartload
Wasser, water	Silber, silver	Theater, theatre
Wetter, weather	Polster, cushion	Zepter, sceptre
Wunder, wonder	Pulver, powder	Zimmer, room
Ruder, oar	Pflaster, plaster	Laster, vice

Manöver, manœuvre
Orchester, orchestra
Register, register
Semester, half-year

41. Nouns beginning with Ge= are generally neuter,

unless they (1) denote living beings (*e.g.*, der Gehilfe, *assistant*) or (2) have a feminine ending (*e.g.*, die Gesellschaft, *company*). The following are exceptions; the first eight (reading across) are masculine, and the rest feminine:

Gedanke, thought	Gesang, hymn
Gefallen, pleasure	Geschmack, taste
Genuß, enjoyment	Gewinn, gain
Gebrauch, custom	Geruch, smell
Gebühr, duty, taxes	Gefahr, danger
Geburt, birth	Geschwulst, swelling
Geduld, patience	Gewähr, security
Gestalt, shape	Gewalt, power

Gebärde, bearing
Gemeinde, community
Genüge, sufficiency
Geschichte, history

[1] Also masculine.

42. Nouns ending in =al or =at are generally neuter, except those denoting persons; *e.g.*, der General, *general*; der Kandidat, *candidate.* Three are feminine: die Moral, *moral*; die Heimat, *native country*; and die Heirat, *marriage*; and the following are masculine:

Kanal, channel	Apparat, apparatus	Spinat, spinach
Pokal, goblet	Muskat, nutmeg	Traktat, treatise
Skandal, scandal	Salat, salad	Monat, month
Vokal, vowel	Senat, senate	Zierat, ornament

43. Nouns ending in =ier are neuter, except der Stier, *bull*; die Gier, *eagerness*; die Manier, *manner*; die Zier, *ornament*; and those denoting persons; *e.g.*, der Offizier, *officer.*

44. Nouns ending in =nis are generally neuter; one is masculine: der Firnis, *varnish*; one can be either feminine or neuter: die or das Versäumnis, *neglect*; and the following are feminine:

Bedrängnis, oppression	Erlaubnis, permission	Kenntnis, knowledge
Befugnis, warrant	Verderbnis, corruption	Kümmernis, grief
Besorgnis, care	Fäulnis, rottenness	Wildnis, wilderness
Betrübnis, grief	Finsternis, darkness	Wirrnis, confusion
Bewandtnis, state, condition		

45. Nouns ending in =sal are neuter; but three are generally feminine: die or das Drangsal, *oppression*; die or das Mühsal, *toil*; and die or das Trübsal, *affliction.*

46. Nouns ending in =tum are neuter, except der Irrtum, *error*, and der Reichtum, *wealth.*

47. Nouns with two genders. The following nouns have two genders with different meanings:

der Band, volume	das Band, ribbon, bond
der Bauer, peasant	das Bauer, cage
der Bund, band, alliance	das Bund, bundle
der Erbe, heir	das Erbe, inheritance
der Flur, entrance-hall	die Flur, field
der Gehalt, contents	das Gehalt, salary
der Heide, heathen	die Heide, heath
der Hut, hat	die Hut, guard
der Kiefer, jaw	die Kiefer, fir
der Kunde, customer	die Kunde, knowledge
der Leiter, guide	die Leiter, ladder
der Mangel, want	die Mangel, mangle
die Mark, mark (coin)	das Mark, marrow
der Marsch, march	die Marsch, marsh
der Messer, measurer, meter	das Messer, knife
der Moment, moment	das Moment, impulse
der Reis, rice	das Reis, twig
der Schild, shield	das Schild, signboard
der See, lake	die See, sea
die Steuer, tax	das Steuer, rudder
der Stift, pin, peg	das Stift, charitable foundation
der Tau, dew	das Tau, rope
der Tor, fool	das Tor, gate
der Verdienst, profit	das Verdienst, merit
die Wehr, defence	das Wehr, weir

PROPER NOUNS

48. Names of persons.

(a) The general rule is that the names of persons add =s in the genitive singular, but otherwise remain unchanged:

Georgs Buch   George's book

(b) Feminine names ending in =e add =s or =ns; but the former is more common:

Maries (or Mariens) Buch   Mary's book

(c) Names ending in a sibilant add an apostrophe or **-ens;** the former is preferable:

Friß' (or Frißens) Buch   Fred's book

(d) Sometimes the case is shown by the definite article; the name is then not inflected: das Buch des (jungen) Georg, (*young*) *George's book*; die Reden des Demosthenes, *the speeches of Demosthenes*; but it is better to say Georgs Buch and Demosthenes' Reden.

(e) If Herr is used before a name, both are declined:

Herrn Schmidts Haus   Mr. Smith's house

(f) With other words denoting title, rank, or relation, the rule is: with the article (or possessive adjective), decline the title but not the name; without it, decline the name but not the title:

König Georgs Söhne	King George's sons
Die Söhne des Königs Georg	The sons of King George
Onkel Wilhelms Haus	Uncle William's house
Das Haus meines Onkels Wilhelm	My Uncle William's house

(g) If Herr and another title are both used with a name, the other title is not inflected; otherwise the rules given in the preceding sections hold good:

Die Meinung des Herrn Professors	The professor's opinion
Die Meinung des Herrn Professor Schmidt, or	The opinion of Professor Smith, or
Herrn Professor Schmidts Meinung	Professor Smith's opinion

(h) Ordinal numbers used as titles must be inflected according to the case of the noun:

Der Hof Wilhelms des Zweiten (Wilhelms II.)   The court of William II

(i) If two or more names come together, only the last is inflected:

Friedrich Wilhelms   Frederick William's govern-
   Regierung   ment

(j) To denote the plural of a surname, ⹀s is generally added. If there is no preposition, the definite article may be used:

Schmidts, die Schmidts   The Smiths
Ich gehe zu Schmidts   I am going to the Smiths'

(k) Jesus Christus becomes Jesu Christi in the genitive and Jesu Christe in the vocative; but the Latin forms of the accusative (Jesum Christum) and dative (Jesu Christo) are no longer much used.

49. Names of places.

(a) Geographical names usually add ⹀s in the genitive singular if they are masculine or neuter, and are invariable if they are feminine:

Die Ufer des Rheins, der   The banks of the Rhine, of
   Donau[1]   the Danube
Die Geschichte Deutschlands The history of Germany

(b) If the name ends in a sibilant, it is not inflected. For *the buildings of Paris* one may say die Gebäude von Paris, or die Gebäude der Stadt Paris, or die Pariser Gebäude. If the name is in apposition, it is not inflected.

(c) If a geographical name is preceded by an adjective, the definite article is used [see paragraph 16 (e)]. When the definite article is used (with or without an adjective), the ⹀s of the genitive singular is sometimes dropped, especially in foreign names:

Die Städte des heutigen   The towns of present-day
   Deutschland(s)   Germany
Die Ufer des Nil(s)   The banks of the Nile

---

[1] Der Fluß is not used with the name of a river; *the River Rhine* is simply der Rhein.

MISCELLANEOUS

50. Nouns of nationality. Most nouns of nationality belong to one of two declensions:

(a) Some end in ـe and are declined like der Knabe [paragraph **26**]. These form the feminine by changing the ـe into ـin, usually modifying, and declined as in paragraph **26** (b):

Der Franzofe, die Franzöſin — The Frenchman, the French-woman

(b) The others end in ـer and are declined like der Onkel [paragraph **23** (a)]. These form the feminine by adding ـin:

Der Engländer, die Engländ-erin — The Englishman, the English-woman

(c) Der Deutſche, *German*, is an exception; it follows the adjectival declensions [paragraphs **142-147**]:

Der Deutſche, ein Deutſcher — The German, a German
Deutſche, die Deutſchen — Germans, the Germans

51. Adjectives of nationality (deutſch, engliſch, etc.) are used as nouns when referring to the language. They are usually spelt with a capital letter, and not declined unless used with the definite article:

Deutſch ſchreiben, lernen — To write, learn German
Auf deutſch, im Deutſchen — In German, in the German
Ins Deutſche überſetzen — To translate into German
Aus dem Deutſchen überſetzen — To translate from German

52. Adjectives used as nouns.

(a) Most adjectives may be used as nouns; they are then written with a capital letter, and follow the adjectival declensions [paragraphs **142-147**]:

Der Fremde, ein Fremder — The stranger, a stranger
Die Fremde, eine Fremde — The stranger, a stranger (*f.*)
Die Fremden, Fremde — The strangers, strangers

(b) Adjectives are used in the same way in the neuter. After das and alles they are declined as in paragraph **145** (weak), and after etwas, nichts, and uninflected viel and wenig they are declined as in paragraph **143** (strong). When ander is used in this construction, it is not spelt with a capital:

Das Gute und das Böse	The good and the evil
Alles Gute, alles Neue	Everything good, everything new
Alles andre	Everything else
Etwas Neues, nichts Neues, viel Neues, wenig Neues	Something new, nothing new, much that is new, little that is new
Mit etwas Neuem	With something new
Mit nichts Gutem	With nothing good

(c) Present and past participles are also used as nouns, as in section (a); *e.g.*, der Reisende, *traveller*; der Gefangene, *prisoner*. They are declined like adjectives [see paragraphs **142-147**].

53. Infinitives may be used as nouns. They are neuter, and are declined like der Onkel [paragraph **23** (a)]:

Das Radfahren wird leicht gelernt	Cycling is easily learnt
Reden ist Silber, Schweigen ist Gold	Speech is silver, silence is gold

54. Collectives. Collective nouns beginning with Ge= are often formed from nouns, or from the stems of verbs, generally with a modification or a change of vowel. They are generally neuter; *e.g.*, das Gebirge, *mountain-range*; das Gebäude, *building*.

55. Diminutives. The suffixes =chen and =lein are used to express smallness, unimportance, familiarity, or affection. Words so formed are generally modified, and are always neuter.

=chen is more common than =lein; but =lein is used after words ending in =ch or =g; *e.g.,* das Büchlein, *booklet.* Sometimes a syllable is dropped; *e.g.,* das Gärtchen, *little garden.*

Sometimes there are two forms with the same meaning —*e.g.,* das Röschen, das Röslein, *little rose*—and sometimes two forms with different meanings; *e.g.,* das Frauchen, *little woman* or *wife* (affectionate); das Fräulein, *young lady.*

56. Feminines ending in =in. A masculine noun is often made feminine by adding =in, generally with a modification; *e.g.,* der Arzt, die Ärztin, *doctor;* der Koch, die Köchin, *cook.*

This change is usual in nouns of nationality [see paragraph **50**], and in nouns formed by adding =er to the stems of verbs; *e.g.,* der Begleiter, die Begleiterin, *companion.*

57. Compound nouns.

Compound nouns are used much more freely in German than in English. When both or all parts of the compound words are nouns, the following are the usual types:

( ) Sometimes the first part of the compound word adds =s to imply a genitive—the dependence of the second part on the first; *e.g.,* der Gottesdienst, *divine service;* der Geburtstag, *birthday.* This form is used with words ending in =heit, =keit, =ion, =schaft, =tät, =tum, and =ung; *e.g.,* die Freiheitsliebe, *love of freedom;* die Zeitungsanzeige, *newspaper advertisement.*

(b) Sometimes =e or =en is added, often as the survival of an obsolete form or of a genitive plural. This form is used with most weak masculines, and with most feminines ending in =e, and with many other nouns; *e.g.,* die Menschenliebe, *philanthropy;* das Tintenfaß, *ink-well.*

(c) Often the first part of the word is not inflected; *e.g.,* der Fußballspieler, *footballer;* der Zahnarzt, *dentist.* This is the usual formation with feminine monosyllables (except die Frau); *e.g.,* der Stadtpark, *municipal park;* der Lastwagen, *lorry.*

Sometimes the final **=e** of a feminine is dropped; *e.g.*, die Erdkunde, *geography*; der Schuljunge, *schoolboy*.

(**d**) Occasionally two forms exist, either with the same meaning—*e.g.*, der Schiff(s)bau, *shipbuilding*—or with different meanings; *e.g.*, der Landmann, *countryman* or *peasant*; der Landsmann, *fellow-countryman*; die Tag(e)arbeit *day-work*; die Tagesarbeit, *day's work*.

(**e**) Verbs, adjectives, and prepositions are often used as the first part of a compound. With verbs, the stem only is generally used; *e.g.*, die Schreibmaschine, *typewriter*.

(**f**) Only the last part of a compound noun is declined; *e.g.*, der Apfelbaum, die Apfelbäume, *apple-tree*.
The gender is usually that of the last word in the compound. Certain exceptions are given in paragraphs **24** (**b**) and **26** (**b**).

58. Order of nouns when used as objects.

(**a**) Normally the dative noun (indirect object) comes before the accusative noun (direct object):

Er hat seinem Vater den Brief gezeigt	He showed his father the letter

(**b**) The indirect object may be put after the direct object for emphasis:

Er hat den Brief seinem Vater gezeigt	He showed the letter to his father

59. Position of the genitive:

(**a**) Normally a noun in the genitive follows the noun on which it depends, except that a proper name in the genitive generally comes first:

Der Bruder meines Freundes	My friend's brother
Heinrichs Bruder	Henry's brother

(b) The genitive is often put first in poetry, and occasionally in prose, even when it depends on a common noun:

Kluger Herren kühne Knechte	Wise lords set their serfs in motion,
Gruben Gräben, dämmten ein,	Dikes upraised and ditches led,
Schmälerten des Meeres Rechte,	Minishing the rights of ocean,
Herrn an seiner Statt zu sein	Lords to be in ocean's stead[1]

60. Nouns in apposition are in the same case. A comma is used as in English:

Ich erkannte meinen Freund, einen jungen Arzt	I recognised my friend, a young doctor
Das ist die Meinung meines Freundes, eines jungen Arztes	That is the opinion of my friend, a young doctor

61. Punctuation. A number of nouns in succession are separated from each other by commas, as in English, but no comma is put before the last one if it is preceded by und:

Vater, Mutter und Kind	Father, mother, and child

---

[1] Bayard Taylor's translation in "The World's Classics."

IV

PRONOUNS

PERSONAL PRONOUNS

62. The personal pronouns are as follows:

First Person	Second Person (*Familiar Form*)	Second Person (*Formal Form*)
Singular:		
N. ich, I	du, thou	Sie, you
A. mich, me	dich, thee	Sie, you
G. meiner, of me	deiner, of thee	Jhrer, of you
D. mir, to me	dir, to thee	Jhnen, to you
Plural:		
N. wir, we	ihr, you	Sie, you
A. uns, us	euch, you	Sie, you
G. unser, of us	euer, of you	Jhrer, of you
D. uns, to us	euch, to you	Jhnen, to you

Third Person Singular

Masculine	Feminine	Neuter
N. er, he	sie, she	es, it
A. ihn, him	sie, her	es, it
G. seiner, of him	ihrer, of her	seiner, of it
D. ihm, to him	ihr, to her	ihm, to it

Third Person Plural

N. sie, they
A. sie, them
G. ihrer, of them
D. ihnen, to them

63. The genitive forms of the third person, seiner and ihrer, are used only of persons. When referring to things, dessen is used for the masculine and neuter singular, and

41

deren for the feminine singular and for the plural (from the demonstrative pronoun der, die, das):

Ich gedenke seiner	I am thinking of him
Ich gedenke dessen	I am thinking of it or of that

64. Use of es. The following uses of es are important:

(a) Es often introduces an intransitive verb in the same way as the English *there* not referring to place. In this construction the verb agrees with the real subject, and in the inverted and transposed orders es is omitted:

Es gehen viele Leute vorbei	There are a great many people walking by
Heute gehen viele Leute vorbei	Today there are a great many people walking by
Obgleich viele Leute vorbeigehen	Although there are a great many people walking by

(b) Es gibt means *there is* or *there are*, and is used in a more general and indefinite sense than es ist and es sind. It is followed by an object, not a subject, and the accusative must therefore be used:

Es sind (or es liegen) zwei Bücher auf dem Tisch	There are two books (lying) on the table
Heutzutage gibt es viele billige Bücher[1]	There are many cheap books nowadays
Es gibt keinen Grund dafür	There is no reason for that

(c) Es is used after a verb to represent a complement or object which may not be expressed in English, or which may be translated by *so*:

Ich glaube (es)	I think so
Er hat nicht geschrieben; er hat es wohl vergessen	He has not written; I suppose he has forgotten

(d) When es is used with the verb sein and another personal pronoun, the English order is reversed:

Ich bin es; ist er es?	It is I; is it he?

[1] The es of es gibt is not omitted in the inverted and transposed orders.

65. Old genitive forms.

(a) The forms mein, dein, and ſein are still occasionally found instead of meiner, deiner, and ſeiner; *e.g.*, das Vergiß=meinnicht, forget-me-not.

(b) An old genitive survives in the form es in such expressions as ich bin es müde, ſatt, zufrieden, *I am tired of it, I have had enough of it, I am satisfied with it.*

66. Da= or dar= with prepositions. With most prepositions [all those in paragraphs **247, 256 (a)** and **270,** except außer, bis, entlang, gegenüber, ohne, and ſeit] da= (dar= before a vowel) is used instead of the personal pronoun in the accusative and dative of the third person when referring to things; *e.g.*, dafür, *for it* or *for them*; darauf, *on it, on them,* or *thereupon*:

Ich weiß nichts von ihm	I know nothing about him
Ich weiß nichts davon	I know nothing about it

67. Translation of 'it.' A masculine or feminine pronoun is often needed to translate *it*:

Hier iſt die Zeitung; ich habe ſie gefunden	Here is the newspaper; I have found it

68. Neuter nouns for living beings. Several feminine English words are represented by neuter German words (das Mädchen, *girl*; das Fräulein, *young lady*; das Weib, *wife, woman.* Das Kind, *child*, and das Geſchöpf, *creature*, may denote people of either sex).

Except das Kind, which is represented by es, these nouns are generally represented by er or ſie, according to the sex of the person mentioned:[1]

Das Mädchen ſaß am Tiſch und las ihr Buch. Bald ſtand ſie auf	The girl was sitting at the table, reading her book. Soon she got up

[1] But if a relative pronoun is used with one of these words as antecedent, it generally follows the strictly grammatical rule: Das Mädchen, das hier iſt, *The girl who is here.*

69. Familiar and formal forms. *You* is translated by bu in elevated and archaic speech; *e.g.*, when addressing God. In everyday speech it is used when addressing (1) a relative, (2) an intimate friend, (3) a boy or girl, (4) an animal. Similarly ihr is used to address two or more people who would be addressed singly with bu.[1] To all other people Sie must be used, being always spelt with a capital. Du and ihr are spelt with capitals in correspondence. For the corresponding possessive adjectives, see paragraph **139**.

70. Personal pronoun not used in English. A personal pronoun is used in German and not in English:

(a) Sometimes when addressing people:

(Du,) Fritz, weißt du . . .?	(I say,) Fred, do you know . . .?

(b) In the first and second person in a relative clause, whether the antecedent is a noun or a pronoun. If the antecedent is in the second person singular, bu in the relative clause may be omitted and the verb put into the third person singular:

Ich, der ich ihn kenne	I who know him
(Du,) mein Freund, der du mich kennst	You, my friend, who know me
(or Du, mein Freund, der mich kennt)	

(c) After wie used as a relative pronoun, a personal pronoun is often supplied as subject or object in the relative clause:

So ein Brief, wie Sie (ihn) geschrieben haben	Such a letter as you have written
Solche Waren, wie (sie) hier zu sehen sind	Such goods as are to be seen here

---

[1] The familiar forms, bu and ihr, are sometimes used in notices and advertisements.

REFLEXIVE, RECIPROCAL, AND EMPHATIC PRONOUNS

71. The reflexive pronouns are as follows. In ſich irren, *to be mistaken*, they are in the accusative, and in ſich ein= bilden, *to imagine*, they are in the dative:

ich irre **mich,** I am mistaken	ich bilde **mir** ein, I imagine
du irrſt **dich**	du bildeſt **dir** ein
er irrt **ſich**	er bildet **ſich** ein
wir irren **uns**	wir bilden **uns** ein
ihr irrt **euch**	ihr bildet **euch** ein
ſie irren **ſich**	ſie bilden **ſich** ein
Sie irren **ſich**	Sie bilden **ſich** ein

Except in the third person (ſich), the reflexive pronouns, accusative and dative, have the same forms as the personal pronouns in the same cases. When ſich is used with the formal form of address (Sie irren ſich), it is still spelt with a small letter.

72. Sich may be either reflexive or reciprocal, but not emphatic ; *e.g.,* ſie mißtrauen ſich may mean *they distrust themselves* or *they distrust each other*. Confusion may be avoided by using the reciprocal pronoun einander, *each other*, or the emphatic pronoun ſelbſt or ſelber, *oneself, myself*, etc. All three are indeclinable:

Wir mißtrauen einander	We distrust each other
Wir mißtrauen uns ſelber	We distrust ourselves
Das hat er ſelber getan	He has done that himself
Er hat ſich verletzt	He has hurt himself

In this connection it is often better to use ſelber than ſelbſt, as ſelbſt is also an adverb meaning *even*.

73. Reflexive instead of personal pronoun. Sometimes the personal pronoun is used in English with reflexive meaning; it must then be translated by the reflexive pronoun:

Er ſah vor ſich hin	He looked in front of him(self)

RELATIVE PRONOUNS

74. The relative pronouns most used are ber and welcher; they both refer to persons and things, and there is no difference in meaning between them. Der is the more common, but welcher is used to avoid too much repetition; *e.g.,* die, welche die Geschichte hörten, *those who heard the story.*[1] They are declined as follows:

	Singular			*Plural*	
	Masc.	*Fem.*	*Neut.*		
N.	der	die	das	die	who, which, that
A.	den	die	das	die	whom, which, that
G.	dessen	deren	dessen	deren	whose, of which
D.	dem	der	dem	denen	to whom, to which

N.	welcher	welche	welches	welche	
A.	welchen	welche	welches	welche	as above
G.	dessen	deren	dessen	deren	as above
D.	welchem	welcher	welchem	welchen	

75. A relative pronoun must agree with its antecedent in gender and number, but its case depends entirely on its relation to the rest of its own clause:

Hier ist der Brief, den ich gestern verloren hatte — Here is the letter that I had lost yesterday

76. Relative clauses are always subordinate. They are therefore separated from the main clause by a comma, and the verb is put last, the auxiliary, if any, being last of all:

Hier ist ein Brief, den ich nicht lesen kann — Here is a letter that I cannot read

Hier ist ein Buch, das ich eben gelesen habe — Here is a book that I have just been reading

[1] Der is always used if the antecedent is a personal pronoun; see paragraph **70 (b).**

77. Position of the relative pronoun.

(a) The usual position of the relative pronoun is next to the antecedent; but it is put later if the sentence would otherwise sound long or awkward:

Ich habe mir die Sache über= legt, von der ich gestern mit Herrn Schmidt sprach	I have thought over the matter that I was talking to Mr. Smith about yester- day

(b) The genitives **dessen** and **deren** come immediately before the noun that they qualify, no article being used:

Ein Haus, in dessen Garten keine Blumen sind	A house in the garden of which there are no flowers

78. Wo= or wor= with prepositions. With most pre- positions [see paragraph **66**] the relative pronoun may (but need not) be replaced by **wo=** (**wor=** before a vowel) when referring to things; *e.g.*, wofür, *for which*; worauf, *on which, whereupon*:

Der Zug, womit (or mit dem) er fährt	The train (that) he is going by

79. Wo is used as a relative adverb in German to introduce a relative clause referring to time or place, as *when* and *where* are used in English:

Das Haus, wo (or worin or in dem) ich wohne	The house where (or in which) I live
In der Zeit, wo[1] (or in der) Karl der Große regierte	At the time when Charle- magne was ruling

80. Wie is used as a relative adverb to denote manner:

Die Art, wie (or in der) er schreibt	The way (in which) he writes

[1] Da was formerly used in this way to mean *when*, but wo is now usual.

81. Weshalb and warum are used as relative adverbs to denote reason:

Der Grund, weshalb (or warum or aus dem) er nicht gekommen ist	The reason (why) he has not come

82. A relative pronoun must not be omitted in German:

Der Herr, mit dem ich sprach	The gentleman (whom) I was talking to
Der Bleistift, den ich verloren habe	The pencil (that or which) I have lost

83. Wer and was as compound relatives.

(a) Wer and was, besides being interrogative pronouns [see paragraph 102], are compound relatives, being used as antecedent and relative pronoun combined, meaning *he who, the one who,* and *what, that which*:

Wer zuletzt lacht, lacht am besten[1]	He laughs best who laughs last
Was ihn betrifft	As for him (literally: what concerns him)

(b) In this construction the demonstrative pronoun, der, die, das, is often used in the main clause for emphasis; it must be used with wer if the cases of the two words are different, as in the second of the following examples:

Was ich denke, das darf ich sagen	What I think, I may say
Wer aber nicht hat, dem wird auch das genommen werden, was er hat[1]	But from him that hath not shall be taken away even that which he hath

84. Was is used as a relative pronoun instead of das:

(a) When the antecedent is a clause:

Im Sommer gehen wir oft schwimmen, was sehr angenehm ist	In summer we often go swimming, which is very pleasant

[1] Wer, used in this sense, means *anyone who*, whereas der, der [see paragraph 88 (b)] may specify a particular person.

(b) After alles, vieles, and nichts:

Alles, was ich habe   All (that) I have

(c) After a neuter adjective (here das is sometimes used):

Das Beste, was (or das) The best thing that can
geschehen kann   happen

85. Desgleichen (masculine and neuter singular) and
dergleichen (feminine singular and plural of all genders)
mean *whose like, the like of whom, the like of which*:

Ein Mann, desgleichen wir   A man whose like we have
nicht gesehen haben   not seen

DEMONSTRATIVE PRONOUNS

86. The demonstrative pronouns are as follows:

     der; derjenige, he, she, it, that, the one
     dieser, this or that, the latter
     jener, that (yonder), the former
     solcher, such
     derselbe, the same
     dergleichen, of that kind

87. Der, when used as a demonstrative pronoun or
adjective [see paragraph 98], is pronounced with a long
closed **e**. It is declined as follows:

| | Singular | | Plural |
	Masc.	*Fem.*	*Neut.*	
N.	der	die	das	die
A.	den	die	das	die
G.	dessen	deren (derer)	dessen	deren (derer)
D.	dem	der	dem	denen

88. Use of der:

(a) Der is often used where a personal pronoun is used
in English:

       Der ist mein Bruder   He is my brother

(b) It is used like the French *celui* before a relative pronoun or genitive in such expressions as *he who, the one who, that of*:

Der, den wir eben gesehen haben[1]	The man (or the one) we have just seen
Meine Bücher und die meines Bruders	My books and my brother's (those of my brother)

(c) It is omitted before an unqualified proper name:

Meine Bücher und Johanns	My books and John's

89. The genitive of der is used instead of the possessive adjective sein or ihr to avoid ambiguity:

Herr A., sein Freund und dessen Junge	Mr. A., his friend, and his (friend's) boy

90. The form derer in the plural and feminine singular of the genitive is used before a relative pronoun or a genitive; otherwise deren is used:

Die Ansichten derer, die gesprochen haben	The views of those who have spoken
Deren (or ihre) Ansichten haben wir schon gehört	We have already heard those people's (or their) views

91. Dies (*this*) **and das** (*this* or *that*) may refer to masculine or feminine nouns, and may be used with a plural form of sein [for a similar use of es and welches, see paragraphs **64** and **107**]:

Das ist meine Schwester, das sind meine Eltern	That is my sister, those are my parents

92. Da= or dar= with prepositions. With most prepositions [see paragraph **66**], the demonstrative pronoun is usually replaced by **da=** (**dar=** before a vowel) when referring to things: dafür, *for that*; darauf, *on that, thereupon*. Similarly hier is used for dies: hierauf, *hereupon*, etc.

---

[1] In the plural, one die sometimes stands for both antecedent and relative; this construction is common in poetry: Die mit Tränen säen, ernten mit Jubel, *They that sow in tears shall reap in joy.*

This construction is not used before a relative pronoun or a genitive:

Ich weiß nichts davon	I know nothing of that (or of it)
Er erinnerte mich daran	He reminded me of that (or of it)
Er erinnerte mich an das, was ich gelesen hatte	He reminded me of what I had been reading
Er verläßt sich auf seine eignen Anstrengungen und auf die seiner Freunde	He relies on his own efforts and on those of his friends

93. Derjenige.

(a) Derjenige is declined as follows:

	Singular		*Plural*
Masculine	*Feminine*	*Neuter*	
N. derjenige	diejenige	dasjenige	diejenigen
A. denjenigen	diejenige	dasjenige	diejenigen
G. desjenigen	derjenigen	desjenigen	derjenigen
D. demjenigen	derjenigen	demjenigen	denjenigen

(b) Derjenige means the same as the demonstrative pronoun der. It is not much used in conversation; in writing it is used for emphasis and to avoid too much repetition of der:

Der (or derjenige), der (or welcher) eben gekommen ist	He (or the one, or the person) who has just come

94. Dieser and jener.

(a) Dieser and jener are declined as follows:

	Singular		*Plural*
Masculine	*Feminine*	*Neuter*	
N. dieser	diese	dieses[1]	diese
A. diesen	diese	dieses[1]	diese
G. dieses	dieser	dieses	dieser
D. diesem	dieser	diesem	diesen

Often shortened to dies.

(b) Dieſer can often be translated by *he* (dieſe by *she*) or *the latter*, and jener by *he* or *the former*; jener is often used in contrast to dieſer:

Frau A. und Frau B. ſprachen miteinander; jene wollte eben Einkäufe machen	Mrs. A. and Mrs. B. were talking to each other; the former was just going shopping

(c) Dieſer and jener must not be used, as pronouns, instead of der or derjenige before a relative pronoun or a genitive [see paragraph **88** (b)]:

Mein Fahrrad und das (or dasjenige) meines Bruders	My bicycle and my brother's

95. Solcher is declined like dieſer [paragraph **94**]:

Das Gemälde als ſolches iſt nicht viel wert	The picture as such is not worth much

96. Derſelbe is declined like derjenige [see paragraph **93**]. It is sometimes used, especially in the commercial and official styles, to mean *he, she,* or *it* (instead of the personal pronoun er, ſie, es, or the demonstrative pronoun der, die, das); but that use should be avoided. It is used correctly as follows:

Dieſes Buch iſt dasſelbe, das ich geſtern las	This book is the same that I was reading yesterday

97. Desgleichen and dergleichen. Compare paragraph **85**. Und dergleichen mehr is shortened to u.dgl.m. [see paragraph **13**], and means *and the like, and so on.* If the reference is to one particular thing in the masculine or neuter singular, desgleichen is used:

Sein erſtes Buch war ein Roman; ſein letztes iſt des= gleichen	His first book was a novel; his latest is of the same kind
Bettler und dergleichen	Beggars and such people

DEMONSTRATIVE ADJECTIVES

98. Demonstrative adjectives. The pronouns given in paragraph **86** are also used as adjectives:

Der[1] Mann	That man
Dasselbe Buch	The same book
Dergleichen Bücher	Books like that (or those)

99. Dieser can often be translated by *that*; jener is generally used in contrast to dieser, or to point out something more remote:

Diese Frage ist nicht leicht zu beantworten	This (or that) question is not easy to answer
Diese Frage ist nicht so leicht zu beantworten wie jene	The latter question is not as easy to answer as the former

100. Solcher is used adjectivally in three constructions:

(a) Before ein it is uninflected. Here it may be replaced by so:

Solch ein Mann (or so ein Mann)	Such a man

(b) After ein it is declined like the adjective in paragraph **146** (mixed declension):

Ein solcher Mann	Such a man

(c) When not used with ein, it is declined like dieser [see paragraph **94**]:

Solche Männer	Such men

101. 'Such' used as an adverb. When *such* is used as an adverb, it is translated by so, or by uninflected solch:

Ein so treuer Hund (or so ein treuer Hund, or solch ein treuer Hund)	Such a faithful dog

---

[1] Pronounced with a long closed *e*.

INTERROGATIVE PRONOUNS

102. The interrogative pronouns are wer, *who*; was *what*; welcher, *which, what*; and was für einer, *what sort (of one)*.

103. Wer and was have no plural. They are declined as follows:

Masc. and Fem.	Neuter
N. wer	was
A. wen	was
G. weffen	weffen
D. wem	(wem)[1]

104. Welcher is declined like diefer [see paragraph **94**], except that it has no genitive.

105. Was für einer is simply was für [see paragraph **112**] used with einer [see paragraph **120**].

106. Direct and indirect questions. The questions in which these pronouns are used may be direct or indirect. If they are indirect, the clause is subordinate, and the verb is put last:

Weffen Haus ift das?	Whose house is that?
Wen haben Sie geftern ge= fehen?	Whom did you see yesterday?
Ich fragte ihn, wen er geftern gefehen habe	I asked him whom he had seen yesterday
Mit welchem von Ihnen hat er gefprochen?	Which of you has he spoken to?

107. Wer, was, and welches may be used with a plural form of the verb fein. Welches is used when referring to a noun of any gender [for a similar use of es and das, see paragraphs **64** and **91**]:

Wer find Ihre Freunde?	Who are your friends?
Welches (or was) find Ihre Gründe?	What are your reasons?

[1] In practice, this form is not used; see paragraph **108**.

108. Wo= or wor= with prepositions. With most prepositions [see paragraph **66**] the interrogative pronoun is replaced by **wo=** (**wor=** before a vowel) when referring to things: wodurch, *through what*; woraus, *out of what*:

Von wem sprechen Sie?	Whom are you talking about?
Wovon sprechen Sie?	What are you talking about?

109. Was instead of warum and wie. Was is sometimes used for warum in questions, and for wie in exclamations:

Was (or warum) eilen Sie so?	Why are you hurrying so?
Was sehen Sie blaß aus! (or Wie blaß sehen Sie aus!)	How pale you look!

INTERROGATIVE ADJECTIVES

110. The Interrogative adjectives are welcher, *which, what,* and was für (ein), *what sort of.*

111. Welcher is declined like dieser [paragraph **94**]. It is used to translate *what* used adjectively:

Welches Buch ist das?	Which (or what) book is that?

112. Was für (ein).

(a) Only the ein is declined, was für remaining unchanged throughout. The ein is, of course, dropped in the plural, which is was für in all cases.

(b) The expression may be split up, was being put before the verb, and für (ein) after the verb:

Was sind das für Blumen? (or Was für Blumen sind das?)	What sort of flowers are those?

(c) The case of ein in this expression depends, not on für, but on the relation of the noun to the rest of the sentence:

Mit was für einer Feder schreiben Sie?	What sort of a pen are you writing with?
Was für ein Baum ist das?	What sort of a tree is that?

113. Welcher and was für (ein) in exclamations:

(a) *What* used with a noun in exclamations is translated by welcher or was für; the adjective, if any, after welcher is declined as in paragraph **145** (weak). The ending of welcher may, however, be dropped, and the following adjective is then declined as in paragraph **146** (mixed):

Welch große Enttäuschungen! What great disappoint-
  (or Welche großen Ent=   ments!
  täuschungen!)

(b) *What a* in exclamations is welch ein (the ending of welcher must be dropped) or was für ein:

Welch eine Enttäuschung! (or   What a disappointment!
  Was für eine Enttäuschung!)

POSSESSIVE PRONOUNS

114. Possessive pronouns. There are four forms of the possessive pronoun in German:

    (a) meiner, mine   uns(e)rer, ours
          deiner, thine   eu(e)rer, yours
          seiner, his   ihrer, theirs
          ihrer, hers   Ihrer, yours

These, and also einer, *one, someone,* and keiner, *nobody,* are declined like dieser [see paragraph **94**].

    (b) der meine   der uns(e)re
          der deine   der eu(e)re
          der seine   der ihre
          der ihre   der Ihre

These are declined like derjenige [see paragraph **93**].

    (c) der meinige   der unsrige
          der deinige   der eurige
          der seinige   der ihrige
          der ihrige   der Ihrige

These are also declined like derjenige.

    (d) mein, unser ⎫
          dein, euer ⎬ as in paragraph **139**, but not
          sein, ihr   ⎪   declined
          ihr, Ihr   ⎭

115. Use of these forms. All these four forms have the same meaning. For ordinary use, forms (a), (b), and (c) are interchangeable, form (a) being the commonest in conversation.

Form (d) is used only as the complement of an intransitive verb such as ſein or werden:

Er hat ſeinen Rock und ich habe meinen (den meinen, den meinigen)	He has his coat and I have mine
Dieſer Rock iſt mein (meiner uſw.)	This coat is mine

116. Special meanings of das Mein(ig)e, die Mein(ig)en, das Dein(ig)e, die Dein(ig)en, etc.:

(a) Das Mein(ig)e means *my part* or *my belongings*:

Er hat das Sein(ig)e getan	He has done his part
Er hat das Sein(ig)e ver= ſchwendet	He has squandered his possessions

(b) Die Mein(ig)en means *my family* or *my friends*:

Die Sein(ig)en ſind zu Hauſe	His people are at home

117. Meinesgleichen, *people like me*, deinesgleichen, etc., are invariable pronouns.

118. Personal for possessive pronoun. In expressions like *a friend of mine* (ein Freund von mir) the Germans use the personal instead of the possessive pronoun.

INDEFINITE PRONOUNS

119. The indefinite pronouns can be divided into two groups:

(a) Those used only as pronouns:

einer } one, someone man	keiner, none, nobody, neither
jedermann, everyone	nichts, nothing
jemand } someone wer	niemand, nobody welcher some

(b) Those used as pronouns and adjectives:

all, all	jeder, jedweder, jeglidher,
ander, other	each, every
beide, both	mancher, some, many, many a
ein bißchen, a little	mehr, more
ein paar, a few	mehrere, several
einige, etliche, some (pl.)	viel, much; *plural*, many
etwas, some (sing.)	wenig, little; *plural*, few
genug, enough	

120. Einer and keiner are declined like the masculine singular of dieſer [see paragraph **94**]. Einer is often used instead of man or jemand, and keiner instead of niemand. For the use of irgend (*e.g.*, irgendeiner, *someone or other*), see paragraph **222**.

121. Jedermann is invariable, except in the genitive, which is jedermanns:

Jedermanns Sache iſt nie=   Everybody's business is no-
    mandes Sache   body's business

122. Jemand and niemand are declined as follows:

N.	jemand	niemand
A.	jemand(en)	niemand(en)
G.	jemand(e)s	niemand(e)s
D.	jemand(em)	niemand(em)

123. Declension and use of man.

(a) Man means *one, they, people, you*, or *we*, according to the context. It has no plural, and for the accusative, genitive, and dative singular the corresponding forms of einer (einen, eines, and einem) are used:

Wenn einem nicht wohl iſt,   If you are (or if one is)
    bleibt man beſſer zu Hauſe   not well, it is better to
                                      stay at home

(b) It is often used instead of the passive:

Man beſchloß alſo, zu Fuß   So it was decided to walk
    heimzukehren   home

(c) It is used with the present subjunctive as a request or suggestion:

Man frage nach dem Prospekt	Please ask for the prospectus
Man vergesse nicht, daß . . .	Let it not be forgotten that . . .

(d) Man must, if necessary, be repeated; it must not be replaced by er. Its possessive adjective is sein:

Man muß arbeiten, wenn man seine Prüfungen bestehen will	You must work if you want to pass your examinations

124. Nichts is indeclinable. For the declension and use of adjectives following nichts, see paragraph **52 (b).**

125. Welcher (singular and plural, declined like dieser, paragraph **94**) and wer (singular, declined as in paragraph **103**) may be used as indefinite pronouns:

Wir haben keinen Tee; ich muß welchen kaufen	We have no tea; I must buy some
Es klopft wer (or einer or jemand)	There is someone knocking

INDEFINITE PRONOUNS AND ADJECTIVES

126. All, whether used as a pronoun or as an adjective, is declined like dieser [see paragraph **94**].

(a) The neuter singular alles means *all, everything,* or *everybody*:

Er erzählte alles, was geschehen war	He told everything that had happened
Alles lief hinaus (or alle liefen hinaus)	Everyone ran out

(b) *All the* is generally translated by inflected all without the article; but it may be translated by uninflected all with the article:

Alle Mühe war vergeblich (or All die Mühe usw.)	All the trouble was in vain

5

(c) Before a possessive or demonstrative adjective, **all** is generally uninflected, especially in the singular:

All fein (biefer) Mut	All his (this) courage
All(e) feine (biefe) Verwandten	All his (these) relatives

(d) In expressions of time involving repetition without variation, **alle** is often used for *every*:

Alle Jahre befuchen wir den= felben Kurort	We go to the same holiday-resort every year
Jebes Jahr befuchen wir einen andern Kurort	We go to a different holiday-resort every year
Alle zwei Jahre, alle brei Jahre	Every other year, every three years

(e) For the declension of adjectives after **all**, see paragraph **147** (b).

(f) *All*, meaning *the whole of*, is generally translated by **ganz**, especially if the thing referred to is regarded as a constant whole.   **Ganz** is invariable when used without the article before the name of a place:

Die ganze Familie	All the family
In ganz England	In the whole of England

(g) Note the use of **alle Welt**:

Alle Welt fpricht fo	Everybody speaks like that
Wer in aller Welt ift bas?	Who on earth is that?

(h) **Alle** is often used colloquially to mean *all gone*:

Die Milch, bas Brot ift alle	The milk, the bread, has all gone

127. Anber.[1]

(a) **Anber** is often used to translate *different* [see the second example in paragraph **126** (d)].

(b) But when no difference is implied, *another* is translated by **noch ein**:

Noch ein Glas Milch, bitte	Another glass of milk, please

---

[1] For the dropping of one **e** in declining **anber**, see paragraph **148**.

(c) *Different from* is anber als; *differently from* is anbers als:

Die Amerikaner haben eine andre Aussprache als die Engländer — The Americans have a different pronunciation from the English

Die Amerikaner sprechen anders als die Engländer — The Americans speak differently from the English

(d) Anber is often best translated by *else* in the expressions alles anbre, etwas anbres, nichts anbres. After jemanb and niemanb, anbers is used.

(e) Anbres, the neuter form of anber, is not the same as anbers, which is an adverb meaning *otherwise* [see paragraph 232].

128. Beibe.

(a) Beibe is generally used to translate *two* when no larger number is concerned:

Meine beiben Brüber — My two brothers
Zwei meiner Brüber — Two of my brothers

(b) The pronoun *both* is often translated by alle beibe:

Alle beibe sinb gekommen — They have both come

(c) When referring to statements or ideas, *both* is often translated by the neuter singular beibes:

Beibes ist richtig — Both (statements) are right

(d) *Both . . . and . . .* (*e.g., both England and Germany; I have both seen and heard it*) is sowohl . . . als . . . [see paragraph 344 (d)].

129. Ein bißchen,[1] ein paar,[1] einige, etliche, and etwas:

(a) Ein bißchen, etwas, and was[2] (which is short for etwas) are singular, ein paar is plural, and einige and etliche are generally plural:

Ein bißchen (or etwas) Brot — A little bread
Ganz (et)was anbres, or (et)was ganz anbres — Something quite different
Es bauerte einige Zeit — It lasted some time (singular)
Einige (or ein paar) Äpfel — A few apples

[1] Indeclinable.　　[2] This shortened form is used only as a pronoun.

(b) Ein paar, *a few*, should be distinguished from ein Paar, a pair; and einige, *a few*, from wenige, *few*:

In einigen (or ein paar) Jahren   In a few years

In wenigen Jahren   In (only a) few years

(c) Etwas and ein bißchen are also used as adverbs. So was and so etwas mean *such a thing*:

Etwas (or ein bißchen or ein wenig) schwer   Rather difficult

So (et)was kann ich nicht verstehen   I cannot understand such a thing

130. Genug, when used as an adjective or adverb, follows the word that it qualifies. For an infinitive following genug, see paragraph **419 (b)**:

Wir haben Zeit genug   We have enough time

Er lief nicht schnell genug   He did not run fast enough

Ich habe genug   I have enough

131. Jeder is much more often used than jedweder and jeglicher. Jeder, whether used as a pronoun or as an adjective, is declined like dieser, except when it is preceded by ein, when it is declined as in paragraph **146** (weak).

Jeden Mittwoch   Every Wednesday

(Ein) jeder bekam ein Geschenk   Everyone received a present

Jeder Schüler weiß das   Any (or every) schoolboy knows that

132. Mancher is declined like dieser [see paragraph **94**]. It is used in the singular (*many a one, many a*) and, less often, in the plural (*many*). If it is followed by an adjective, it may drop the ending and remain manch, and the adjective is then declined as in paragraph **144** (strong); but if mancher is declined, the adjective that follows is declined as in paragraph **145** (weak):

Manches alte Gebäude (or manch altes Gebäude)   Many an old building

Manche alten Gebäude (or manch alte Gebäude)   Many old buildings[1]

---

[1] *Many* is generally better translated by viele, which is stronger than manche.

133. Mehr and mehrere. Mehr is indeclinable. Mehrere is declined like the plural of dieser [see paragraph **94**]. Like beide [see paragraph **128**], it is sometimes used as a pronoun in the neuter singular:

Ein Baum mit mehr Frucht, mehr Blättern	A tree with more fruit, more leaves
Ein Garten mit mehreren Bäumen	A garden with several trees
Wir haben mehreres gesehen	We have seen several things

134. Viel and wenig are sometimes declined and sometimes not. They may be declined like dieser [paragraph **94**] when used as pronouns, and like adjectives [see paragraphs **142-146**] when used as adjectives. Inflection is often optional; the following is a general guide:

(a) Both are declined after der or a possessive adjective:

Das wenige Geld, das er hat	The little money that he has
Sein weniges Geld	His little (stock of) money

(b) In the plural, both are inflected, always as pronouns, and generally as adjectives:

Viele (Leute) sind gekommen	Many (people) have come

(c) In the singular, both may be inflected or uninflected, whether as pronouns or as adjectives. As adjectives, they are generally uninflected:

Vielen Dank	Thank you very much
Viel Vergnügen	I hope you will enjoy yourself
Viel Glück	Good luck
Viel Geld	Plenty of money
Wir haben viel(es) gesehen	We have seen a great deal

(d) Ein wenig is indeclinable:

Mit ein wenig (or ein bißchen or etwas) Geduld	With a little patience

(e) Both are indeclinable when used as adverbs:

Er arbeitet viel (wenig)   He works a great deal (little)

(f) For declension of adjectives after viel and wenig, see paragraph **147**.

POSITION OF PRONOUNS

135. Position of pronouns used as direct and indirect objects:

(a) Personal pronouns come before other pronouns:

Ich habe ihm das nicht ge=   I have not given him that
geben

(b) Of two personal pronouns, the accusative comes first:

Ich habe es ihm nicht gegeben   I have not given it to him

This rule is sometimes disregarded by putting **'s** (for es) after a dative: ich will dir's zeigen, *I will show it you.*

(c) A pronoun comes before a noun, whether it is accusative or dative:

Ich will es meinem Bruder   I will show it to my brother
zeigen
Ich will ihm das Buch zeigen   I will show him the book

(d) In the inverted and transposed orders, a personal or reflexive pronoun used as an object is sometimes put before a noun subject. There is no hard and fast rule about this; it depends on the balance of the sentence. The following example is slightly abbreviated:

Da er nun ganz arglos bei den Netzen saß, kam ihn ein un=
vorhergesehener Schrecken an, als er es im Waldesdunkel
rauschen hörte, wie Roß und Mann, und sich das Geräusch
immer näher nach der Landzunge herauszog.

V

ADJECTIVES

136. Demonstrative adjectives. See paragraphs **98** ff.

137. Interrogative adjectives. See paragraphs **110** ff.

138. Indefinite adjectives. See paragraphs **126** ff.

POSSESSIVE ADJECTIVES

139. Possessive adjectives. The following are the possessive adjectives with the corresponding personal pronouns:

ich, I	mein, my	wir, we	unſer, our
du, thou	dein, thy	ihr, you	euer, your
er, he	ſein, his	ſie, they	ihr, their
ſie, she	ihr, her	Sie, you	Ihr, your
es, it	ſein, its		

140. Declension. The possessive adjectives, and also ein, *a*, and fein, *no*, are declined as follows:

	Masculine	*Feminine*	*Neuter*	*Plural*
N.	mein	meine	mein	meine
A.	meinen	meine	mein	meine
G.	meines	meiner	meines	meiner
D.	meinem	meiner	meinem	meinen

141. Use of the possessive adjectives:

(a) They must, of course, agree with the noun that they qualify:

Seine Feder (*feminine*)	His pen
Ihr Bleiſtift (*masculine*)	Her pencil
Ihre Bleiſtifte (*plural*)	Her (or their) pencils

(b) The gender and number of the noun to which they refer must be kept in mind:

Meine Uhr hat ihren Sekun= denzeiger verloren	My watch has lost its second-hand
Das englische Volk und sein Parlament	The English people and their Parliament

(c) With das Fräulein, *young lady*, ihr is used [see paragraph **68**]:

Das Fräulein trägt ihren neuen Hut	The young lady is wearing her new hat

(d) All the possessive adjectives form compounds like meinerseits, *for my part*; meinetwegen, *for my sake, for all I care*; um meinetwillen, *for my sake*.

(e) For the use of the definite article instead of the possessive adjective (*e.g., He has broken his arm*), see paragraph **16** (**g**).

DECLENSION OF ADJECTIVES

142. Adjectives are declined in different ways, according to whether or not they are preceded by a determining word (*i.e.*, by an article or by one of certain pronominal adjectives).

143. Strong declension. If no determining word precedes, the adjective is declined as follows:

	Singular	
Masculine	*Feminine*	*Neuter*
good wine	good ink	good glass
N. guter Wein	gute Tinte	gutes Glas
A. guten Wein	gute Tinte	gutes Glas
G. guten Weines	guter Tinte	guten Glases
D. gutem Weine	guter Tinte	gutem Glas

Plural (All Genders)

N. gute Weine, Tinten, Gläser
A. gute Weine, Tinten, Gläser
G. guter Weine, Tinten, Gläser
D. guten Weinen, Tinten, Gläsern

144. Genitive ending. The ending =es is occasionally used in the masculine and neuter singular genitive, instead of =en; but the latter is more common.[1] With this exception, the endings of the strong declension are the same as those of dieser [see paragraph **94**].

145. Weak declension. If the adjective is preceded by der, dieser, jeder, or jener, or by an inflected form of mancher, solcher, or welcher, it is declined as follows:

Singular

Masculine	*Feminine*	*Neuter*
the good wine	the good ink	the good glass
N. der gute Wein	die gute Tinte	das gute Glas
A. den guten Wein	die gute Tinte	das gute Glas
G. des guten Weines	der guten Tinte	des guten Glases
D. dem guten Weine	der guten Tinte	dem guten Glase

Plural (All Genders)

N. die guten Weine, Tinten, Gläser
A. die guten Weine, Tinten, Gläser
G. der guten Weine, Tinten, Gläser
D. den guten Weinen, Tinten, Gläsern

146. Mixed declension. If the adjective is preceded by ein, mein, dein, sein, unser, euer, ihr, Ihr, or kein, it is declined as follows:

---

[1] The ending =es would be preferred if the genitive case were not shown by the noun (*e.g.*, in the genitive of guter Mensch), but this is rare.

Singular

Masculine	Feminine	Neuter
no good wine	no good ink	no good glass

N. fein guter Wein   feine gute Tinte   fein gutes Glas
A. feinen guten Wein feine gute Tinte   fein gutes Glas
G. feines guten Weines feiner   guten   feines   guten
                   Tinte   Glases
D. feinem guten Weine feiner   guten   feinem   guten
                   Tinte   Glase

Plural (All Genders)

N. feine guten Weine, Tinten, Gläser
A. feine guten Weine, Tinten, Gläser
G. feiner guten Weine, Tinten, Gläser
D. feinen guten Weinen, Tinten, Gläsern

147. After certain other words, adjectives are declined as follows:

(a) After uninflected viel, wenig, manch, solch, and welch, as in paragraph **143** (strong):

Viel gutes Wasser   Plenty of good water

(b) After inflected all, as in paragraph **145** (weak):

Alle großen Häuser   All (the) big houses

(c) After viele, wenige, andre, einige, and mehrere, as in paragraph **143** (strong):

Viele große Häuser   Many big houses
Die Zimmer vieler großer The rooms of many big
  Häuser   houses

(d) After a personal pronoun an adjective is generally strong in the singular and weak in the plural:

Du englischer Schüler   You English schoolboy
Wir englischen Schüler   We English schoolboys

148. Adjectives ending in =e, =el, =en, and =er.

(a) Adjectives ending in =e always drop the =e when inflected:

Ein leiſes Klopfen   A soft tapping

(b) Adjectives ending in =el usually drop the e when inflected, and those ending in =en and =er sometimes do so:

Ein ed(e)les Gemüt   A noble mind
Ein heit(e)res Gemüt   A cheerful mind
Trock(e)nes Wetter   Dry weather

(c) Adjectives ending in =el and =er usually take the endings =eln, =erm, and =ern, instead of =len, =rem, and =ren; *e.g.*, edeln, heiterm, heitern.

149. The adjective hoch, *high,* drops the e when inflected:

Ein hoher Berg   A high mountain

150. Adjectives following the noun, or used predicatively, are not inflected:

Das Haus iſt leer   The house is empty
Das Haus, alt und leer, iſt   The house, old and empty,
  zerfallen   is in ruins

151. Adjectives joined by a hyphen. Of two or more adjectives joined by a hyphen, only the last is declined:

Die   National=Sozialiſtiſche   The National-Socialist Party
  Partei

152. Adjectives used in pairs. A few adjectives, such as groß und klein, alt und jung, are used in pairs without inflection and with a singular verb:

Jung und alt verſammelte   Young and old gathered
  ſich draußen   outside

153. Adjectives are formed from the names of towns by adding ⸗er; they are spelt with a capital letter, and are indeclinable:

> Die Berliner Schulen　　　The schools of Berlin

154. Adjectives of nationality. See paragraph **51.**

COMPARISON OF ADJECTIVES

155. Comparison of adjectives. Adjectives generally form the comparative by adding ⸗er, and the superlative by adding ⸗st. In doing so, some adjectives of one syllable modify the vowel [see list in paragraph **157**]:

> lang　　länger　　der, die, das längste　　long
> klar　　klarer　　der, die, das klarste　　clear

156. Adjectives ending in ⸗e, ⸗el, ⸗en, ⸗er, or a vowel or ⸗h:

(a) Adjectives ending in ⸗e add only ⸗r in the comparative:

> weise　　weiser　　der, die, das weiseste　　wise

(b) Adjectives ending in ⸗el, ⸗en, or ⸗er usually drop this ⸗e in the comparative:

> edel　　edler　　der, die, das edelste　　noble

(c) Adjectives ending in a vowel other than ⸗e, or in ⸗h preceded by a vowel, usually add ⸗st in the superlative.

> treu　　treuer　　der, die, das treu(e)ste　　faithful
> froh　　froher　　der, die, das froh(e)ste　　happy

(d) Adjectives ending in ⸗d, ⸗t, or a sibilant add ⸗est in the superlative:

> hart　　härter　　der, die, das härteste　　hard
> heiß　　heißer　　der, die, das heißeste　　hot

157. Modification of vowel in the comparative and superlative.

(a) The following adjectives modify in the comparative and superlative:

arg, bad	dumm, stupid	flug, clever
grob, coarse	jung, young	fur3, short
groß, big	hart, hard	frank, ill
alt, old	falt, cold	arm, poor

lang, long	scharf, sharp
(oft, often)[1]	schwar3, black
gesund, healthy	schwach, weak
warm, warm	stark, strong

(b) The following are generally modified in the comparative and superlative:

bang, anxious	farg, niggardly
blaß, pale	schmal, narrow
glatt, smooth	rot, red

158. The following comparisons are irregular:

groß	größer	der, die, das größte	big
gut	beffer	der, die, das beste	good
hoch	höher	der, die, das höchste	high
nah(e)	näher	der, die, das nächste	near
viel	mehr[2]	der, die, das meiste	much
wenig	{minder[2]	der, die, das mindeste}	little
	{weniger[2]	der, die, das wenigste}	

159. Declension. Comparative and superlative adjectives must be declined like positives when used before a noun:

Die Ausficht wird flarer	The view is getting clearer
Eine flarere Ausficht	A clearer view

---

[1] Adverb only. [2] Indeclinable.

160. Superlative with am. Though the positive and comparative may be used without article or inflection, the superlative must not.[1] If the superlative is used as a predicate without implying a comparison between the thing qualified and other things of the same kind, the stem of the superlative takes the ending **=en,** and is preceded by am:

Im Januar ist das Wetter kalt, kälter, am kältesten	The weather is cold, colder, coldest in January

If a comparison with other things of the same kind is implied, the form given in paragraph **155** must be used:

Der Monat Januar ist der kälteste	The month of January is the coldest

161. 'Most,' when no comparison is implied, must be translated by an adverb, not by the superlative:

Er ist sehr (or höchst or äußerst) höflich	He is very (or most) polite

162. 'Most,' when used with a plural noun, is **die meisten:**

Die meisten Bücher	Most (of the) books
Die meisten meiner Freunde	Most of my friends

With a singular noun, *most* has to be paraphrased:

Der größte Teil des Buches	Most of the book

163. 'Somewhat,' or **'rather,'** followed by a noun and adjective, may be translated by the comparative, instead of by **etwas:**

Er macht eine längere Reise	He is taking a rather long journey

164. A repeated comparative adjective is generally translated by **immer** with the comparative:

Die Tage werden immer länger, immer schwüler	The days are getting longer and longer, more and more sultry

---

[1] For uninflected superlative adverbs, see paragraph **205.**

But the comparative is sometimes repeated (länger und länger) in German, as in English. *More and more*, standing alone, is mehr und mehr.

165. Comparison of equals and unequals.

(a) Wie is used after the positive, and als after the comparative:

A. ift (eben)fo flug (nicht fo flug) wie B.	A. is as clever (not as clever) as B.
A. ift (nicht) flüger als B.	A. is (not) cleverer than B.

(b) *Than as* is denn als:

Er handelte mehr als Soldat denn als Staatsmann	He acted more as a soldier than as a statesman

166. Use of mehr in comparisons. When two qualities of the same person or thing are compared, mehr is used with the positive form of the adjective:

Er ift mehr träge als dumm	He is lazy rather than stupid (more lazy than stupid)

167. Comparisons of inferiority are made with weniger, *less*:

Diefe Überfetzung ift weniger richtig als jene	This translation is less correct than that

168. Nichts weniger als is generally translated by *anything but*:

Er ift nichts weniger als dumm	He is anything but stupid

169. For comparison of adverbs, see paragraphs **201-208.**

CASES USED WITH CERTAIN ADJECTIVES

170. Adjectives taking the genitive, dative, or accusative. Many adjectives govern one of these cases. They need cause little difficulty, as the English equivalent is generally a good guide. In German, the adjective generally follows the noun that it governs, as in the examples given below:

(a) The following adjectives take the genitive:

bar, free or devoid of
bedürftig, in need of
bewußt, conscious of
eingedenk, mindful of
fähig, capable of
gewahr, aware of
gewärtig, expectant of
gewiß, sure or certain of
kundig, acquainted with
mächtig, master of

müde, tired of
satt,[1] satiated with
schuldig, guilty or deserving of
sicher, secure or certain of
teilhaftig, participating in
überdrüssig, disgusted with
verdächtig, suspected of
verlustig, deprived of
wert[1] ⎱ worthy of
würdig ⎰

Ich bin Ihrer (des Krieges, der Predigt) müde	I am tired of you (of the war, of the sermon)
Dessen ist er nicht fähig	He is not capable of it

(b) The following adjectives take the dative:

abgeneigt, averse to or from
ähnlich, similar to
angemessen, suitable or adequate to
angenehm, agreeable to
behilflich, helpful to
bekannt, (well) known to
dankbar, grateful to
eigen, peculiar to
fremd, strange to
gehorsam, obedient to
geneigt, well disposed, subject, liable to
gewogen, well disposed to

gleich, equal or indifferent to
lästig, troublesome to
möglich, possible to
nah(e), near to
nützlich, useful to
schädlich, harmful to
treu, faithful to
überlegen, superior to
verantwortlich, responsible to
verbunden, obliged to
willkommen, welcome to
zugetan, attached or devoted to

Das ist mir (ihm, meinen Eltern) nicht angenehm	That is not agreeable to me (to him, to my parents)
Ich bin Ihnen (Ihrem Bruder) sehr verbunden	I am much obliged to you (to your brother)

[1] Also takes the accusative

(c) Expressions of measurement followed by an adjective are in the accusative.

The adjectives los, *rid of*, and gewohnt, *accustomed to*, are used with the accusative or, less often, the genitive:

Einen Fuß hoch, tief, lang, breit	A foot high, deep, long, broad
Einen Monat alt	A month old
Er ist mir den Betrag schuldig	He owes me the amount
Ich bin ihn, den Mann (or seiner, des Mannes) los	I am rid of him, of the man

171. For adjectives followed by certain prepositions, see paragraphs 289–305.

USE OF PARTICIPLES AS ADJECTIVES

172. Present and past participles are often used as adjectives. [For their use as nouns, see paragraph **52 (c)**.] When they are followed by a noun, they must be declined in the ordinary way:

Der Fliegende Holländer	The Flying Dutchman
Der eben angekommene Zug	The train that has just come in

When the English participial form is part of a tense, it must not be treated as an adjective:

Der Junge lacht (lachte)	The boy is laughing (was laughing)

For a similar distinction in past participles, see paragraph **451 (b)** on the passive voice.

PUNCTUATION

173. Punctuation.

(a) If two or more adjectives are used before a noun, all but the last are followed by a comma:

Ein großes, helles, geräumiges Zimmer	A big, light, spacious room

(b) But if the last adjective and the noun form together a single idea which the preceding adjective limits, they are not preceded by a comma:

Die großen deutschen Flüsse   The big German rivers

(c) If the last two adjectives are joined by und or oder, no comma is put between them:

Ein großes, helles und geräu-   A big, light, and spacious
miges Zimmer   room

NUMERALS AND MEASUREMENTS

CARDINAL NUMBERS

174. The cardinal numbers are as follows:

1 ein(s)	14 vierzehn	70 siebzig
2 zwei	15 fünfzehn	80 achtzig
3 drei	16 sechzehn	90 neunzig
4 vier	17 siebzehn	100 hundert
5 fünf	18 achtzehn	120 hundert(und)=
6 sechs	19 neunzehn	zwanzig
7 sieben	20 zwanzig	221 zweihundert=
8 acht	21 einundzwanzig	einundzwanzig
9 neun	22 zweiundzwanzig	1,000 tausend
10 zehn	30 dreißig	1,101 eintausendein=
11 elf	40 vierzig	hundertundeins
12 zwölf	50 fünfzig	1,000,000 eine Million
13 dreizehn	60 sechzig	2,000,000 zwei Millionen

175. Tausend is not generally used in dates: das Jahr neunzehnhundertsechsunddreißig, *the year 1936.*

176. Slight irregularities are to be noticed in the numbers 16, 17, 30, 60 and 70.

177. Compound numbers of hundreds, tens, and units (*e.g.*, zweihunderteinundzwanzig) are usually written as one word.

178. Ein.

(a) The form eins is used in counting. When a noun is used or implied, ein must be declined as in paragraph **18**: Wieviele Briefmarken haben Sie? How many stamps have —Ich habe nur eine you?—I have only one

(b) Ein may be preceded by der; it is then declined as in paragraph **145** (weak):

Der eine, der andre   The one, the other
Die einen, die andern   Some, the others

(c) E i n, when spaced for emphasis [see paragraph **10**], always means *one*; otherwise it may mean *a*:

Ich habe nur eine Postkarte   I have only had a post-
bekommen   card
Ich habe nur e i n e Post=   I have only had one postkarte bekommen   card

(d) Einer [declined like dieser, paragraph **94**], besides being an alternative to man [see paragraph **123**], is used as a pronoun in a more definite sense:

Einer (eine) von uns   One of us
Ich habe einen der Briefe   I have lost one of the letters
verloren

(e) If the word ein comes last as part of a larger number, the following noun is singular:

Nach hundertundeinem Tage   After a hundred and one
                               days

179. 'One' or 'ones,' used as pronouns after an adjective, must not be translated:

Dies ist ein gutes Ei, das ist This is a good egg, that is a
ein schlechtes   bad one

180. Inflection of numbers above ein. Numbers above ein are invariable, except that zwei and drei may add =er in the genitive to show the case, and occasionally =en in the dative:

Die Meinung dreier Zeugen   The opinion of three wit-
(or von drei Zeugen)   nesses
Zu zweien, zu zweit   By twos (or in pairs)
Zu dreien, zu dritt   By threes

181. Die Zwanziger, *the twenties;* die Dreißiger, *the thirties*, etc., apply to age and to dates:

Er ist in den Vierzigern   He is in the forties

182. Hundert means *a hundred*; einhundert, *one hundred*; and so with tausend. These words may also be used as neuter nouns declined like das Jahr [see paragraph **24 (b)**]:

Da waren Hunderte von Menschen	There were hundreds of people there
Zu Tausenden	By thousands

183. Use of =erlei, =fach and =mal.

(a) **=erlei** means *kinds of*; words with this ending are invariable:

Er hat zweierlei Socken an	He has odd socks on

(b) **=fach** means *-fold*; einfach means *plain, simple*, or *single*. Words with this ending are declined:

Eine einfache Fahrkarte	A single (not return) ticket
Ein vierfaches Versprechen	A fourfold promise

(c) **=mal** means *times*. Words with this ending are invariable, but form adjectives by adding **=ig:**

Noch einmal, bitte	Once more, please
Nicht einmal eine Mark	Not even a shilling
Eine dreimalige Reise	A journey that was made three times

184. Fractions.

(a) Fractions are formed by adding **=tel** to the cardinal numbers from 4 to 19 inclusive (except that acht gives das Achtel), and **=stel** to those from 20 onwards. The words so formed are neuter nouns declined like der Onkel [see paragraph **23 (a)**]:

Drei und vier Fünftel	Three and four-fifths
Neunzehn Zwanzigstel	Nineteen-twentieths

(b) *The half* is die Hälfte; *the third* is das Drittel:

Die erste Hälfte des Buches	The first half of the book
Ein Drittel des Kuchens	A third of the cake

(c) The adjective *half* is halb, used after the article. With names of places used without the article, halb is not inflected:

Eine halbe Stunde	Half an hour
Halb England	Half England

(d) =einhalb (invariable) may be used with the cardinal numbers to translate *and a half*.[1]

Ein(und)einhalb Kilometer	One and a half kilometers
Zwei(und)einhalb Pfund	Two and a half pounds
In drei(und)einhalb Stunden	In three and a half hours

(e) Das Viertel, *quarter*, is joined to the noun in such expressions as die Viertelstunde, *quarter of an hour*; das Viertelpfund, *quarter of a pound*; it is also used as in section (b) above.

(f) The decimal point is expressed in German by a comma. The comma is therefore not generally used, as in English, to separate groups of thousands, but a space is often left instead:

5,9 (fünf komma neun)	5.9
2 167 459	2,167,459

ORDINAL NUMBERS

185. The ordinal numbers below 20 (except those meaning *first*, *third*, and *eighth*) are formed by adding =t to the corresponding cardinal number; from 20 onwards they are formed by adding =st. They are used as pronouns or adjectives as in English, and are declined like the adjectives in paragraphs **142-146**. When the number is a compound one, only the last part of the cardinal is changed into an ordinal:

1st	der erste	8th	der achte
2nd	„ zweite	9th	„ neunte
3rd	„ dritte	10th	„ zehnte
4th	„ vierte	100th	„ hundertste
5th	„ fünfte	101st	„ hundert(und)erste
6th	„ sechste	120th	„ hundert(und)zwanzigste
7th	„ siebente[2]	221st	„ zweihunderteinundzwanzigste

[1] The following alternative forms are less generally used: 1½, anderthalb; 2½, drittehalb; 3½, viertehalb.

[2] Der siebente is better than der siebte, which is sometimes used.

186. The ordinal numbers are always inflected :[1]

Er ist der vierte in seiner Klasse	He is fourth in his class
Im zweiten Stock	On the second floor

187. To write ordinals as figures, write the cardinal number and add a full stop:

Am 31. (einunddreißigsten) Juli	On the 31st July

188. For the word 'time' after an ordinal number, =mal or das Mal[2] is used:

Das erstemal or das erste Mal	The first time
Zum drittenmal or zum dritten Mal	For the third time

189. For 'firstly,' 'secondly,' etc., =ens is added to the stem of the ordinal:

Erstens, zweitens, drittens	Firstly, secondly, thirdly

EXPRESSIONS OF TIME

190. Time of day.

(a) Hours (die Stunde, *the hour*):

Wieviel Uhr ist es?	What time is it ?
Wie spät ist es?	What time is it ?
Was ist die Uhr?	What time is it ?
Es ist ein,[3] zwei, drei Uhr	It is one, two, three o'clock
Um drei Uhr	At three o'clock
Gegen drei Uhr	About or towards three o'clock
Gerade (or eben) drei Uhr	Exactly (or just) three o'clock
Der Mittag, die Mitternacht	Midday, midnight

[1] Except that in such expressions as *second largest*, zweit=, dritt=, viert=, etc., are used: die zweitgrößte Stadt, *the second largest town*.

[2] For the difference between das Mal and die Zeit, compare this example with the second in paragraph **79**.

[3] If *o'clock* is not translated, eins is used: zwanzig (Minuten) nach eins, *twenty (minutes) past one*.

(b) Fractions of hours:

Eine halbe Stunde	Half an hour
Eine Viertelstunde	A quarter of an hour
Drei Viertelstunden	Three-quarters of an hour
(Ein) Viertel nach drei, or (Ein) Viertel (auf) vier	A quarter past three
Zwanzig (Minuten) nach drei	Twenty (minutes) past three
Halb vier, halb eins	Half past three, half past twelve
Zwanzig (Minuten) vor vier	Twenty (minutes) to four
(Ein) Viertel vor vier, or Drei Viertel (auf) vier	A quarter to four

(c) Morning, evening, etc.:

Morgens, nachmittags, abends, nachts[1]	In the morning, afternoon, evening, night
Heute früh or heute morgen, heute nachmittag, heute abend[2]	This morning, this afternoon, this evening or tonight
Guten Morgen, guten Tag, guten Abend, gute Nacht	Good morning, good day or good afternoon, good evening, good night

(d) Figures and time-tables. German time-tables use the 24-hour clock; 6.45 p.m. is 18⁴⁵.

Apart from time-tables, quarter and half hours are generally written as follows if figures are used:

$$\left.\begin{array}{ccc} \tfrac{1}{4}4, & \tfrac{1}{2}4, & \tfrac{3}{4}4, \\ & \text{or} & \\ 3\tfrac{1}{4}, & 3\tfrac{1}{2}, & 3\tfrac{3}{4}, \end{array}\right\} \quad 3.15, \quad 3.30, \quad 3.45$$

191. Use of cases in expressions of time. Indefinite expressions of time are generally in the genitive, and definite ones in the accusative, unless am is used:

---

[1] See alternative forms in paragraph **191** (a) and (c).
[2] Or diesen Morgen, diesen Nachmittag, etc.

(a) Genitive. Notice the inflection of die Nacht:

Des Morgens, des Nachmittags, des Abends, des Nachts	In the morning, afternoon, evening, night (not generally referring to one particular day)
Des Sonntags, des Montags usw.[1]	On Sundays, Mondays, etc.
Eines Tages	One day (past or future)

(b) Accusative:

Jeden Abend, jeden Freitag	Every evening, every Friday
Diesen Abend, heute abend	This evening
Nächsten Freitag	Next Friday
Den nächsten (folgenden, andern) Tag	The next day
Den ganzen Tag	All day, the whole day
Warten Sie einen Augenblick	Wait a moment

(c) With prepositions:

Am Morgen, am Nachmittag, am Abend, am Tage	In the morning, afternoon, evening, in the daytime (by day)
In der Nacht	In the night
Bei Tag, bei Nacht	By day, by night
Am nächsten (folgenden, andern) Tage	(On) the next day
Heute in acht (vierzehn) Tagen, or Heute über acht (vierzehn) Tage	Today week (fortnight)
Heute vor acht (vierzehn) Tagen	A week (fortnight) ago

192. Translation of 'for.' Für is generally not used in expressions of time.

(a) Während, *during*, may be used of past, present, or future time:

Während der nächsten Tage habe ich viel zu tun	I have a great deal to do for the next few days

[1] Or sonntags, montags usw.

(b) Past time:

Er arbeitete drei Monate lang[1]	He worked for three months
Ich habe ihn drei Monate (or seit drei Monaten) nicht gesehen	I have not seen him for three months
Einige Minuten schwieg er	For a few minutes he was silent

(c) Past and present time. Note the difference of tense according to meaning, and see paragraph **441** (c):

Er arbeitet schon drei Monate (or seit drei Monaten) hier	He has been working here for three months (and is still doing so)
Er hat drei Monate (lang) hier gearbeitet	He worked here for three months (and is no longer doing so)

(d) Future time:

Er reist auf drei Monate nach Berlin	He is going to Berlin for three months

193. Translation of ' when.'

(a) If it is a question, either direct or indirect, use wann:

Wann fährt der Zug ab?	When does the train leave?
Ich weiß nicht, wann der Zug abfährt	I do not know when the train leaves

(b) Referring to a single occasion or period in past time, use als:

Als er jung war, spielte er Fußball	When he was young, he used to play football

---

[1] In this construction lang is used, but the usual adverbial form is lange: Das hat lange gedauert, *That has lasted a long time.*

(c) Referring to present or future time, or to repeated occasions in the past, use wenn:

Wenn (sobald) es schön ist, werden wir spazieren gehen	If or when (as soon as) it is fine, we shall go for a walk
Wenn es schön war, gingen wir spazieren	When it was fine, we went (*i.e.*, we used to go) for a walk
(Jedesmal,) wenn es schön war (or sooft es schön war), gingen wir spazieren	Whenever it was fine, we went for a walk

(d) For *when* used as a relative adverb (*e.g., at the time when Charlemagne was ruling*), see paragraph **79.**

DATES, AGES, ETC.

194. Dates. Ordinal numbers are used, as in English. *On the 1st January* is either am 1. (ersten) Januar (dative) or den 1. (ersten) Januar (accusative). *In 1900* is either im Jahre 1900 or simply 1900:

Der wievielte ist heute? (or Den wievielten haben wir heute?)	What is the date today?
Es ist der 30. Juni (or Wir haben den 30. Juni)	It is the 30th June
Am 30. Juni (or den 30. Juni)	On the 30th June
Am Freitag, dem 30. Juni	On Friday, the 30th June
Im Juni	In June
Luther wurde (im Jahre) 1483 geboren	Luther was born in (the year) 1483

195. Addresses. In heading letters, the town is generally written first; then the name of the street, followed by the number of the house, and, if necessary, of the floor; then the date in the accusative:

Lübeck,
  Augustusstraße, 37ᴵᴵ,
    d. 30. Juni, 1936

    2nd floor,
      37 Augustus Street,
        Lübeck,
          30th June, 1936

196. Age is expressed as in English:

Wie alt sind Sie?	How old are you?
Ich bin achtzehn (Jahre alt)	I am eighteen (years old)

197. Nouns of measurement of length, weight, value, etc.

(a) These are generally uninflected (except feminine nouns ending in *-e*). *Of* is generally not translated, the two nouns being in apposition, and therefore taking the same case:[1]

Zwei Glas Milch	Two glasses of milk
Zwei Dutzend Eier	Two dozen eggs
Mit zwei Dutzend Eiern	With two dozen eggs
Eine Menge Leute	A crowd of people
Zwei Tassen Tee	Two cups of tea
50 000 Mann	50,000 men (*e.g.*, in an army)

(b) *Of* is generally translated if the noun is preceded by an article or a pronominal or possessive adjective (*this, your*, etc.):

Zwei Glas von dieser Milch	Two glasses of this milk

(c) When used in an adverb phrase without a preposition, the noun is in the accusative:

Das Lineal ist einen Fuß lang	The ruler is a foot long

198. Distributive expressions.

(a) In phrases like *two shillings a pound, sixpence a yard*, the definite article is used with the noun in the accusative:

Zwei Mark das Pfund	Two shillings a pound
Fünfzig Pfennig das Meter	Sixpence a yard

---

[1] If the second noun is preceded by an adjective, it is usually in the genitive; see paragraph **266 (a)**.

(b) In similar expressions referring to time, **in** with the dative is often used:

Zweimal im Jahre, im Monat,   Twice a year, month, week
in der Woche (or Zweimal
das Jahr, den Monat, die
Woche)[1]

(c) *Each* in such expressions is generally **je** or **Stück**:

Apfelsinen zu je zehn Pfennig   Oranges at a penny each
(or Apfelsinen zu zehn
Pfennig das Stück)

[1] Similarly in expressions of speed: achtzig Kilometer **in der** Stunde (or achtzig Kilometer die Stunde), *fifty miles an hour.*

VII

ADVERBS AND ADVERB PHRASES

FORMATION AND COMPARISON OF ADVERBS

199. Formation of adverbs.

(a) Some adverbs are formed by joining together, or by adding suffixes to, other parts of speech; *e.g.*, deshalb, *therefore*; teils, teilweise, *partly*; freilich, *certainly*; erstens, *firstly*.

(b) Some are not compounded or borrowed from other parts of speech; *e.g.*, jetzt, *now*; dann, *then*; hier, *here*.

(c) Most are adjectives used as adverbs; *e.g.*, schlecht, *bad(ly)*; schnell, *quick(ly)*; amtlich, *official(ly)*.

200. Adjectives used as adverbs. Most adjectives (including participles used as adjectives) are used as adverbs without inflection:

Eine leicht geschriebene Aufgabe	An easily written exercise
Eine überraschend schnelle Reise	A surprisingly quick journey
Er sprach sehr aufgeregt	He spoke very excitedly

201. Comparison of adverbs. The ordinary superlative of adverbs is different from that of adjectives [see paragraph **155**]. The following is the normal adverbial comparison:

scharf	schärfer	am schärfsten	sharply
klar	klarer	am klarsten	clearly

Er spricht klar, klarer, am klarsten	He speaks clearly, more clearly, most clearly (*i.e.*, more clearly than anyone else)[1]

[1] See paragraph **204**.

202. For adverbs ending in **e, ⸗el, ⸗en, ⸗er,** or a vowel or **⸗ḥ,** and for the modification of the vowel in comparisons, see paragraphs **156** and **157.**

203. Irregular comparisons. The following adverbs, besides those given in paragraph **158,** are irregular in their comparison:

balb	{ eḥer	am eḥeſten	} soon
	{ früḥer	am früḥeſten	
gern(e)	lieber	am liebſten	willingly
woḥl	beſſer	am beſten	well

204. The superlative adverb, when no definite comparison is intended, must be translated either with the help of a second adverb such as ſeḥr or ḥöcḥſt [see paragraph **161** for a similar construction with adjectives] or by aufs followed by the superlative adjective:

Er ſpricḥt ſeḥr (or ḥöcḥſt or äußerſt) klar   He speaks very or most clearly

Er ſpricḥt aufs klarſte   He speaks in the clearest possible way

Er ſpricḥt am klarſten   He speaks more clearly than anyone else

205. Superlative adverbs ending in ⸗ſt. The following superlatives ending in ⸗ſt are used without any additional ending:

(a) in **⸗ig** and **⸗licḥ:** eiligſt, *in all haste*; gütigſt, *most kindly*; freundlicḥſt, *most kindly* or *most pleasantly*; ḥöflicḥſt, *most respectfully* or *most politely*:

Sie wollen micḥ gütigſt ent⸗ ſcḥulbigen   You will be so kind as to excuse me

(b) Ḥöcḥſt and äußerſt, *extremely*; meiſt, *mostly, for the most part*; längſt, *long since*:

Dieſe Ḥerren ſinb meiſt(ens) Engländer   These gentlemen are mostly English

(c) Möglicḥſt is used to mean *as . . . as possible*:

Laufen Sie möglicḥſt ſcḥnell   Run as quickly as possible

206. Superlatives ending in -ens.

(a) Besides the adverbs in -ens formed from numerals [see paragraph **189**], the following are common: beſtens (Danke beſtens, *Thank you very much*); höchſtens, *at the most*; meiſt(ens), *for the most part*; nächſtens, *very soon*; ſpäteſtens, *at the latest*; mindeſtens and wenigſtens, *at least*.

(b) Mindeſtens and wenigſtens. Wenigſtens denotes a restriction; either may denote a minimum:

Vor mindeſtens (or wenig-ſtens) drei Tagen	At least three days ago
Er kommt bald; das ſagt er wenigſtens	He is coming soon; at least, he says so

207. Comparison of equals and unequals.

(a) As with adjectives [see paragraph **165**], wie is used after the positive, and als after the comparative:[1]

Er kann (eben)ſo gut ſchreiben (Er kann nicht ſo gut ſchrei-ben) wie ſein Bruder[2]	He can write as well (He cannot write as well) as his brother
Er kann beſſer ſchreiben als ſein Bruder[2]	He can write better than his brother

(b) When the subject in the clause of comparison is a pronoun representing the subject of the main clause, and the verb is one of the modal auxiliaries, wie is often omitted:

Er ſprach, ſo ſchnell er konnte, durfte, wollte	He spoke as fast as he could, was allowed to, wanted to

208. Immer, mehr, and weniger may be used with adverbs as with adjectives [see paragraphs **164, 166, 167,** and **168**].

---

[1] A few adverbs—*e.g.*, weit, *far*—may be followed by wie or als in the positive.

[2] As wie and als introduce abbreviated clauses, they follow the main clause; but they are not preceded by a comma unless they introduce a complete clause with subject and verb.

VARIOUS ADVERBS

209. Alſo means *therefore*, not *also*. Often it can be best translated by *so*, and in conversation it is sometimes used for *well*, *then*, or *now*:

Alſo blieb ich zu Hauſe	So I stayed at home
Alſo leſen Sie weiter	Go on reading, then

210. Auch.

(a) **Auch** generally means *also*, *too*, or *even*:

Dieſes Haus iſt auch zu ver= kaufen	This house is for sale, too
Auch dieſes Haus iſt zu ver= kaufen	This house, too (or Even this house), is for sale[1]
Ich bin müde.—Ich auch	I am tired.—So am I

(b) In a negative sentence it often translates *nor*, *neither*, or *either*:

Ich bin nicht müde.—Ich auch nicht	I am not tired.—Nor am I (or Neither am I, or I am not, either)

(c) **Auch** or **immer** is used after **wer, was, wo,** and **ſo** or **wie,** to mean *whoever*, *whatever*, *wherever*, and *however* respectively. These expressions are used as subordinating conjunctions like **wenn auch** [see paragraph **338**], and the verb therefore comes last:

Wer, was, wo es auch (or immer) iſt (ſein mag)	Whoever, whatever, wherever it is (may be)
So (or wie) kalt es auch iſt	However cold it is
Wer auch Ihr Freund iſt	Whoever your friend is

(d) *Wherever*, implying one place, is **wo auch**, as in the preceding paragraph. If it implies several places, it is **überall, wo**:

Überall, wo ſie zu finden ſind	Wherever they are to be found

---

[1] *Even* could be expressed more strongly by **ſelbſt** or **ſogar**.

7

(e) Wenn auch means *although* or *even if* [see paragraph 338].

(f) Auch and zu. Auch means *too* in the sense of *also*. *Too*, implying degree, is zu:

Das ist auch leicht	That is easy, too
Das ist zu leicht	That is too easy

211. Bald means *soon.* Bald . . ., bald . . . (used at the beginning of a sentence and repeated) means *now . . ., now . . .; now . . ., then . . .; sometimes . . ., sometimes . . .,* etc.:

Bald dies, bald das	First this, then that
Bald lief er fort, bald kam er wieder	Now he would run off, then he would come back

212. Da.

(a) Da, when used as an adverb, can generally be translated by *there, then, so,* or *and.* Occasionally it need not be translated:

Da haben Sie recht	There you are right
Da (or dann) ging er fort	Then he went off
Da (or also) ging er fort	So he went off
Ich sagte es ihm, da lachte er	I told him, and he laughed
Als ich es ihm sagte, da lachte er	When I told him, he laughed

(b) Da is also a conjunction meaning *as* or *since* in the sense of *because* [see paragraph **325**]. If, as generally happens, da comes first in the sentence, the inverted order means that it is an adverb, and the transposed order generally means that it is a conjunction:

Da haben Sie recht	There you are right
Da Sie recht haben	As or since you are right

(c) For the use of da as a relative adverb, see paragraph **79** (note).

(d) For the use of da as a pronoun, see paragraphs **66** and **92.**

213. Dann, denn,[1] and damals.

(a) Dann means *then* in the sense of *at that time* (generally referring to the future), or *after that*, or *in that case*:

Dann wird er 21 Jahre alt sein	He will then (*e.g.*, next month) be 21 years old
Dann (or da) sprach er wieder	Then he spoke again
Dann dürfen Sie bleiben	You may stay, then

(b) Denn means *then* in the sense of *well then, why*, or *so*:

Was ist denn los?	Well, what is the matter?
Wie kommt das denn?	Why, how is that?

(c) Denn is used in geschweige denn, *still less, much less*, and in es sei denn, daß, *unless*. Es sei denn, daß is less common than wenn nicht [see paragraph **339**]:

Er kommt gewiß, wenn er nicht krank ist (or es sei denn, daß er krank ist)	He is sure to come, unless he is ill
Er kann kaum schwimmen, geschweige denn tauchen	He can hardly swim, let alone (or still less) dive

(d) Damals means *at that time*, referring to the past:

Damals wohnten wir hier	We were then living here

214. Doch has many shades of meaning. The following are examples of the commonest uses:

(a) *But, yet, after all, you know, surely, why*:

Sie kennen ihn doch?	Surely you know him?
Das ist doch kaum möglich	Why, that is hardly possible
Und doch hat er nichts gesagt	And yet he said nothing
Er ist doch nicht gekommen	He has not come, after all
Aber Sie haben es doch selber gesagt	But you said so yourself, you know

(b) To express a wish or emphasis:

Hätte er doch (or nur) geschrieben!	If only he had written!
Kommen Sie doch (or nur) herein!	Do come in!

---

[1] For benn as a conjunction, see paragraph **312**.

(c) To mean *yes* (like the French *si*) after a question in the negative:

Haben Sie das nicht gehört?	Have you not heard that ?—
—(O) doch	(Oh) yes

(d) It is sometimes used as a co-ordinating conjunction meaning *but*, put at the beginning of a sentence and not causing inversion:

Ein Geschlecht geht dahin, und ein anderes kommt, doch die Erde bleibt ewig bestehen	One generation passeth away, and another generation cometh, but the earth abideth for ever

(e) A less common construction is the use of doch after the verb and subject (inverted order) instead of the conjunction denn, *for*: Hab ich doch nicht verleugnet . . . (Luther), For I have not denied . . .

215. Eben generally means *just* (not *even*, except as an adjective):

Ich bin eben (or gerade) fertig	I have just finished
Das kann ich eben nicht sagen	I really can't tell you
Das ist eben, was er sagte	That is just what he said

216. =ein and =in. =ein or ein= (*e.g.*, eintreten, *to enter*) imply movement; =in implies no movement:

Was ist darin?	What is in it ?
Was haben Sie hinein gelegt?	What have you put in it ?

217. Erst is often best translated by *only*, though its most obvious meaning is *first*. Conversely, *only* in expressions of time is translated by erst, not by nur. (This does not apply to expressions of duration of time; *e.g.*, *It lasted only ten minutes* is Es dauerte nur zehn Minuten.) *First of all* is generally zuerst or zunächst:

Zuerst möchte ich sagen	I should like to say first
Er kommt erst um sechs Uhr	He is not coming till six o'clock
Er ist erst zehn Jahre alt	He is only ten years old
Erst recht, erst recht nicht	All the more, less than ever

218. Genug and zu. In expressions like *old enough to do it*, or *too old to do it*, the *to* is expressed by um zu or zu [see paragraph **419** (**b**)]:

Er ist zu vorsichtig, (um) einen solchen Fehler zu machen	He is too careful to make such a mistake

219. Gern and lieber. Gern means *willingly*, and lieber *more willingly*. They should generally be used in translating such expressions as *I like, I should like, I am fond of, I prefer*. The spelling gerne is often used:

Essen Sie gern Eier?	Do you like eggs?
Trinken Sie gern Kaffee?	Do you like coffee?
Rauchen Sie gern Zigarren?	Do you like cigars?
Noch eine Tasse Tee, bitte.— Ja, gerne	Another cup of tea, please.— Yes, with pleasure
Er möchte (gern) kommen	He would (very much) like to come
Er möchte lieber zu Hause bleiben	He would rather (or He would prefer to) stay at home
Sie bleiben lieber (or besser) hier	You had better stay here

220. Her and hin.

(**a**) Her (*hither*) implies movement towards, and hin (*thither*) implies movement away from, the person or thing concerned. They are sometimes used alone, but are more often joined to prepositions and used as separable prefixes [see paragraphs **456** ff.]:

Kommen Sie herein	Come in(side)
Gehen Sie hinein	Go in(side)
Er geht ins Zimmer (hinein)	He goes into the room
Er kam heraus	He came out
Eine Stimme kam von unten her	A voice came from down below
Er sah vor sich hin	He looked in front of him

(**b**) Her is used in expressions of time such as:

Das ist schon lange her	That is a long time ago now
Das ist schon einen Monat her	That is a month ago already
Von jeher	From time immemorial

(c) Hin is used to mean *lost, gone,* or *exhausted*:

Alles ist hin	All is lost (or gone)
Mein Geld ist hin	My money has all gone

(d) Her and hin are used with adverbial accusatives such as:

Er kam den Fluß herab	He came down the river
Er ging den Berg hinauf	He went up the hill

(e) Hin und her means *to and fro, hither and thither*; hin und wieder, *now and then*; hin und zurück, *there and back.*

(f) Herum and umher. Herum means *round in a circle*; umher means *in all directions, on all sides*:

Der Kreisel dreht sich herum	The top spins round
Der Mann blickt umher	The man looks all round him

(g) With hier, *here*; da or dort, *there*; and wo, *where*, her or hin must be added if movement to or from a place is implied (daher generally means *therefore*):

Wo sind Sie?	Where are you?
Wohin gehen Sie? (or Wo gehen Sie hin?)	Where are you going to?
Woher kommen Sie? (or Wo kommen Sie her?)	Where do you come from?
Er ist hier	He is here
Er kommt (hier)her	He is coming here

221. Irgend is often used with the indefinite article, and also with pronouns and adverbs, to mean *any (at all)*:

Irgendeine Zeitung	Any newspaper you like
Irgendeiner, irgend etwas	Anyone, anything you like
Irgendwie, irgendwo	Somehow, somewhere or other

222. Ja.

(a) Ja does not always mean *yes*. An emphatic *yes* is often jawohl, or ja, ja, or, in contradictions, doch. Ja, unemphasised at the beginning of a sentence, is generally *well* [compare nun, paragraph **227**]:

Wie denken Sie darüber?—	What do you think about it?
Ja, das muß ich mir erst überlegen	—Well, I must think it over first

(b) Ja is often used to emphasise a statement or request:

Das ist ja möglich	That is certainly possible
Ich habe es ja schon gesehen	I have seen it already, you know
Kommen Sie ja!	Mind you come!

(c) It is often put at the end of a question to suggest an affirmative answer:

Sie gehen gleich nach Hause, ja?	You are going straight home, aren't you?

223. Kaum, *scarcely*, may be followed by da or so and a main clause, or by als and a subordinate clause:

Kaum hatten wir ihn gesehen, da (or so) lief er ins Haus (or als er ins Haus lief)	We had scarcely seen him when he ran into the house

224. Mal, short for einmal, is often used in conversation much as the English use *just*:

Sagen Sie mal	Just tell me

225. Nämlich and namentlich. Nämlich means *namely, you see, you know, as a matter of fact*; namentlich means *especially*:

Das Wetter war kalt, es war nämlich Winter	The weather was cold; you see, it was winter
Wir bekommen oft Regen, namentlich (or besonders) im Winter	We often have rain, especially in winter

226. Noch. The general meaning is *still*; other translations are often necessary:

Er schläft noch	He is still asleep
Noch nicht, noch nie	Not yet, never yet
Noch einmal	Once more
Noch einmal so viel	As much again
Noch gestern, noch morgen	Only yesterday, tomorrow at the latest [else?
Sonst noch etwas?	(Would you like) anything
Noch ein Glas Milch, bitte	Another glass of milk, please.

227. Nun and jetzt. Both mean *now*, and may refer to an account of past events. Nun also means *now* or *well* without reference to time:

Nun (or jetzt) fing es an zu regnen	It now began to rain
Nun, wie geht's?	Well, how are you?
Es ist jetzt halb elf	It is now half past ten

228. Nur.

(a) Nur means *only* [see paragraph **217** for *only* translated by erst]:

Ich sehe ihn nur selten	I see him only rarely

(b) It is also used for emphasis, as in the following examples:

Kommen Sie nur herein	Do come in
Wenn ich ihn nur gesehen hätte	If only I had seen him
Warten Sie nur	(You) just wait
Was soll ich nur sagen?	Whatever am I to say?

229. Schon means *already*. Other possible translations are *now, ever, yet, surely*:

Das habe ich schon gehört	I have heard that already
Er ist schon zwei Monate (or seit zwei Monaten) dort	He has been there two months now
Die Gelegenheit wird sich schon finden	The chance will come, you may be sure
Haben Sie das schon gelesen?	Have you read that yet? (or Have you ever read that?)

230. Sehr is generally used to translate *very much* used with a verb, if it denotes degree rather than quantity:

Es ärgerte ihn sehr	It annoyed him very much
Danke sehr	Thank you very much

231. So.

(a) So can generally be translated by *as, so,* or *such*:

So groß wie	As big as
Nicht so groß wie	Not as (or so) big as
Das Wetter war so schlecht	The weather was so bad
So ein Mann wie er	Such a man as he

(b) Sometimes it is used for slight emphasis:

So recht	Quite right, exactly
So ziemlich	Fairly

(c) It is often used as a non-committal answer to a statement, and can then generally be translated by *Yes?, Oh, Really, Indeed,* or some such remark.

(d) It is often used to introduce a main clause after a clause of condition [see paragraph **337 (b)**]; it is then not translated.

(e) It does not translate *so,* meaning *therefore.* Also, daher, or darum are generally used:

Es wurde spät, also ging ich schlafen	It was getting late, so I went to bed

(f) For so . . . auch, meaning *however* and introducing a clause of concession, see paragraph **210 (c)**.

232. Sonst and anders.

(a) Both are used with the meaning *else* after jemand, *somebody,* and niemand, *nobody:*

Jemand anders (or sonst jemand)	Someone else

(b) When used to qualify verbs, sonst means *or else, in different circumstances;* anders means *in a different way:*

Anders kann ich nicht handeln	I cannot act differently
Sie müssen mir trauen, sonst kann ich nicht handeln (or oder ich kann nicht handeln)	You must trust me, or I cannot act

233. Wo.

(a) In main sentences, wo is an interrogative adverb:

Wo ist er?	Where is he?

(b) For the use of wo as a pronoun, relative adverb, and subordinating conjunction, see paragraphs **78, 108, 79,** and **341** respectively.

234. Wohl and gut.

(a) Wohl and gut both mean *well*. Gut is generally used to express *well* when it directly modifies a verb (*e.g.*, Er schreibt gut, *He writes well*), though *Farewell* is Leben Sie wohl. Sie haben gut reden, lachen usw. means *It is all very well for you to talk, laugh*, etc.

(b) Wohl is often used, without emphasis, to express probability:

Das ist wohl richtig, aber es gehört nicht hierher	That is no doubt true, but it is not the point
Sie wissen wohl, daß er nicht kommt?	I suppose you know that he is not coming?

235. Prepositions used as adverbs.
Sometimes a preposition is used as an adverb to give greater force to one already used:

Der Blick von meinem Zimmer aus	The view from my room
Von nun an	From now on(wards)

NEGATIVES

236. Negatives.

(a)

Nicht, not	nein, no (to a question)
gar nicht, not at all	kein, no (not a)
nicht mehr, no more or no longer	gar kein . . ., no . . . at all
	kein . . . mehr, no more . . .
nichts, nothing	keiner, niemand, nobody
nie (mals), nimmer, never	nirgend(s), nirgendwo, no-where
noch nicht, not yet	
noch nie, never yet	

Ich habe ihn noch nie gesehen	I have never yet seen him
Das ist gar nicht leicht	That is not at all easy
Ich habe gar keine Tinte	I have no ink at all
Er kann nicht mehr schlafen	He cannot sleep any more (or any longer)
Ich habe keine Tinte mehr	I have no more ink

(b) *But*, meaning *except* after a negative, is als:

Nichts als die Wahrheit	Nothing but the truth
Keiner als mein Freund	Nobody but my friend
Nirgends als in diesem Zim= mer	Nowhere but in this room

(c) Nicht wahr? (often shortened to nicht?) corresponds to the French *n'est-ce pas?* and the translation depends on the person, number, and gender of the preceding subject:[1]

Das ist leicht, nicht (wahr)?	That is easy, isn't it?
Sie haben den Brief ge= schrieben, nicht (wahr)?	You have written the letter, haven't you?

237. Redundant negative. Such constructions as Ich darf nicht gehen, ehe ich nicht die Aufgabe geschrieben habe, *I must not go before I have written the exercise,* are no longer common. The redundant negative is, of course, for emphasis, and is found among the best German writers.

238. Sondern and aber. The conjunction *but* is trans- lated by sondern when it connects two contrary terms or statements the first of which is negatived:

Es ist nicht kalt, aber es regnet	It is not cold, but it is raining
Es ist nicht kalt sondern warm	It is not cold, but warm
Das ist kein Fehler, aber dieser Satz ist besser	That is not a mistake, but this sentence is better
Das ist kein Fehler sondern gutes Deutsch	That is not a mistake, but good German

239. Position of nicht. The usual positions of nicht are as follows:

(a) If it negatives the predicate as a whole, nicht is put last, except for an infinitive, a past participle, or a pre- dicative noun or adjective:

Arbeiten Sie heute nicht?	Are you not working today?
Haben Sie heute nicht ge= arbeitet?	Have you not been working today?

[1] Gelt? is often used instead of nicht wahr? in South Germany.

Ich kann meine Aufgabe nicht finden	I cannot find my excercise
Das ist nicht meine Aufgabe	That is not my exercise
Das ist nicht richtig	That is not correct

(b) Nicht comes before any word or phrase (other than the finite verb) that it specially qualifies. It generally comes before an adverbial expression of manner or place:

Nicht alles, was man hört, ist richtig	Not all that one hears is true
Er arbeitet nicht fleißig	He does not work hard
Heute ist er nicht in der Schule	He is not at school today

POSITION OF ADVERBS AND ADVERB PHRASES

240. Position of adverbs and adverb phrases.

(a) In a main sentence the subject must not be separated from the finite verb, as is often done in English:[1]

Er stand bald wieder auf (or Bald stand er wieder auf)	He soon stood up again

(b) If two or more adverbial expressions occur, the usual order is time, manner, place:

Ich fahre morgen mit dem Dampfer nach Rostock	I am going to Rostock by steamer tomorrow

(c) Adverbs follow pronouns:

Ich kann das leicht tun	I can easily do that

(d) If a sentence contains an adverbial expression and a noun object, the more emphatic of the two generally follows:

Wir erreichten bald die Stadt	We soon reached the town
Wir erreichten die Stadt gegen halb elf	We reached the town about half past ten

[1] This rule often has to be applied in translating sentences where *and* is followed by an adverb; thus, *He lay down and soon went to sleep* is Er legte sich hin und schlief bald ein, or Er legte sich hin und bald schlief er ein.

(e) An adverbial expression generally precedes a predicative adjective, unless it is a prepositional phrase limiting the adjective, when it generally follows:

Das Wetter ist im Januar kalt	The weather is cold in January
Er ist stolz auf seinen Hund	He is proud of his dog

241. Adverbs beginning a sentence.

(a) Adverbs and adverb phrases are often put at the beginning of a sentence. The inverted order is then used, the subject following the verb:

Bald stand er wieder auf	Soon he stood up again
Morgen fahre ich mit dem Dampfer nach Rostock	Tomorrow I am going to Rostock by steamer
Gegen halb elf erreichten wir die Stadt	About half past ten we reached the town

(b) If an adverb is used with the subject and regarded as part of it, the inverted order is not used:

Auch das ist möglich	That, too, is possible

(c) An adverb like nun or freilich may be put at the beginning of a sentence and followed by a comma without causing inversion:

Nun (freilich), das kann wahr sein	Well (certainly), that may be true

(d) An adverb and an adverb phrase, or two adverbs not forming a phrase, are not usually put together at the beginning of a sentence:

Dann sah ich ihn einige Tage später auf der Straße	Then, a few days later, I saw him in the street

(e) In exclamations, both the inverted and the transposed orders are used:

Wie froh war ich! (or Wie froh ich war!)	How glad I was!

242. Punctuation. Adverbs and adverb phrases are not separated by commas from the rest of the sentence:[1]

Troɧ des ſchlechten Wetters reiſte er früh ab	In spite of the bad weather, he set off early

ADVERBIAL GENITIVE AND ACCUSATIVE

243. Adverbial genitive.

(a) For expressions of time in the genitive, see paragraph **191** (a).

(b) The adverbial genitive of place is not common. Examples of the adverbial genitive of degree and manner are:

dritter Klaſſe, third class	glücklicherweiſe, fortunately
trocknen Fußes, dryshod	vorzugsweiſe, for preference
meines Erachtens, in my opinion	allerdings, certainly
meines Wiſſens, as far as I know	keineswegs, by no means

244. Adverbial accusative.

(a) For the adverbial accusative of time and measurement, see paragraphs **191** (b) and **197** (c).

(b) The accusative of place or direction is used in such constructions as:

Wir ſegelten den Fluß hinab (hinauf)	We sailed down (up) the river
Er ging ſeinen Weg[2]	He went on his way

---

[1] Exceptions are: (1) adverbs used as in paragraph **241(c)**; (2) phrases with (an)ſtatt . . . zu, ohne . . . zu, and um . . . zu (Er ſtand auf, um hinauszugehen, *He got up to go out*); (3) participial constructions [see paragraph **244 (c)**].

[2] Er ging ſeines Weges or ſeiner Wege means that he went on in his own way, without regard to other people's views.

(c) The accusative is used in absolute constructions, often with a past participle. If a participle is used, the phrase is separated from the rest of a sentence by a comma:

Den Stock in der Hand ging er weiter	(With) his stick in his hand, he went on
Seinen Blick auf den Boden gerichtet, ging er weiter	(With) his gaze fixed on the ground, he went on

VIII

PREPOSITIONS

245. Cases used after prepositions. German prepositions govern (*a*) the accusative, (*b*) the dative, (*c*) the accusative or dative, (*d*) the genitive.

246. Certain prepositions may govern the dative or genitive, generally without any difference of meaning; these are indicated by *.

Others either may or must follow the word that they govern; these are indicated by †.

PREPOSITIONS GOVERNING THE ACCUSATIVE

247. The following prepositions govern the accusative:

bis, as far as	gegen, against, towards
durch, through	ohne, without
†entlang, along	um, round
für, for	wider against

248. Bis.

(*a*) Bis is often used with other prepositions; *e.g.*, an, nach, or zu:

Er ging bis an die Tür	He went as far as the door
Er fuhr bis nach Hamburg, bis zum Rathaus	He went as far as Hamburg, as far as the town-hall
Ich bleibe bis zum 10. März	I am staying till the 10th March

(*b*) Bis is used without another preposition (1) referring to names of places when no action (such as walking there) is emphasised, and (2) in expressions of time not involving dates (when it sometimes means *by*):

Bis Lübeck war der Weg gut	The road was good as far as Lübeck
Er bleibt bis Montag	He is staying till Monday
Ich will es Ihnen bis Montag mitteilen	I will let you know by Monday

(c) Bis auf may mean (1) *as far as, up to, including*, or (2) *except*:

Bis auf weiteres	Till further notice
Sie verschwanden bis auf den letzten	They all disappeared, down to the last (man)
Sie verschwanden bis auf einen	They all disappeared except one

Confusion may be avoided by using ausgenommen or außer, instead of bis auf, for *except*.

(d) Bis is generally used for *or* in such expressions as zwei bis drei, *two or three*.

(e) *Not till* is generally translated simply by erst; see paragraphs **217** and **324**.

249. Durch and the passive. The following examples show the difference between durch, mit, and von when used with the passive:

(a) Von expresses an active agency such as a man or a horse:

Der Brief wurde von meinem Bruder geschrieben	The letter was written by my brother

(b) Durch expresses a more general or less individual agency, such as weather or illness:

Er wurde durch eine Erkältung verhindert	He was prevented by a cold

(c) Mit expresses an instrument used by an active agent:

Der Brief wurde mit einer Feder geschrieben	The letter was written with a pen

8

250. Entlang generally follows the word that it governs. It is rarely used with the genitive or dative:

Er ging die Straße entlang   He walked along the street

251. Für.

(a) Für is not generally used in expressions of time; see paragraph **192**.

(b) Für is not a conjunction. *For*, used as a conjunction, is denn:

Hier ist ein Brief für Sie   Here is a letter for you
Ich weiß nicht, was er sagt,   I don't know what he is say-
   denn ich kann ihn nicht   ing, for I can't hear him
   hören

(c) It means *by* in such expressions as:

Tag für Tag, Schritt für   Day by day, step by step,
   Schritt, Stück für Stück   piece by piece

252. Gegen and wider. Wider, unlike gegen, expresses only hostile relations:

Gegen acht Uhr   Towards (or about) eight o'clock

Seine Güte gegen ihn   His kindness to(wards) him
Gegen (or wider) den Wind   Against the wind
Gegen Berlin ist Kiel nur   Kiel is only small compared
   klein   with Berlin

253. Um.

(a) Um, referring to place, is often followed by herum, which causes no change of meaning:

Sie saßen um den Tisch herum   They were sitting round the table

(b) Um, referring to time, means *at* [see paragraph **191** (a)]:

Um acht Uhr   At eight o'clock

(c) Referring to measurements of all kinds, um means *by* in such constructions as:

Länger um zwei Meter	Two yards longer
Der Preis ist um eine Mark gestiegen (gefallen)	The price has gone up (gone down) by a shilling

254. Ausgenommen is a past participle, sometimes used as a preposition meaning *except.* It may precede or follow the word that it governs. It may take either the accusative or the same case as the word qualified by the phrase:

Die ganze Klasse, ein (or einen) Schüler ausgenommen, ist hier	The whole class is here, except one boy

255. Gen, towards, is rarely used, except in poetical language in such expressions as gen Himmel, *heavenwards.*

PREPOSITIONS GOVERNING THE DATIVE

256. The following prepositions govern the dative. Those in paragraph (a) are the commonest:

(a)

aus, out of	seit, since
außer, besides, except	von, of, from, about
bei, near, with, among	zu, to, at
mit, with	†gegenüber, opposite
†nach, to, after, according to	

(b)

*binnen, without	nebst } together with
dank, thanks to	samt
†entgegen, opposite	ob, beyond
†gemäß, according to	*†zufolge, in consequence of
*längs, along	†zuwider, contrary or repugnant to
nächst, next to	

257. Aus generally means *out of* or *from*. The following are examples of its commonest uses:

(a) To express movement from a place:

Er lief aus dem Zimmer	He ran out of the room

(b) To express origin, referring to time, place, or material:

Moden aus dem 18. Jahrhundert	Fashions from the 18th century
Er kommt aus Leipzig	He comes from Leipzig
Das Haus ist aus Stein	The house is made of stone

(c) To express a cause:

Aus seiner Antwort schloß ich, daß . . .	I inferred from his answer that . . .
Aus diesem Grunde	For that reason
Aus Schwäche	From weakness
Aus Versehen	By mistake

(d) It is used adverbially to mean *out* or *finished*:

Das Feuer, das Licht ist aus	The fire, the light is out
Er lief zur Tür hinaus	He ran out at the door
Die Stunde ist aus	The lesson is over

258. Außer.

(a) Außer means *except* or *besides*:

Keiner außer ihm	Nobody except (or besides) him

(b) It also means *outside, out of, beyond*:

Außer Gefahr, außer Frage	Out of danger, out of the question
Außer sich vor Freude	Beside oneself for joy
Außer Zweifel	Beyond doubt
Hauptmann außer Dienst (generally written a.D.)	Retired captain

259. Bei.

(a) Bei means *by*, *near*, or *beside*:

Schwartau bei Lübeck	Schwartau, near Lübeck
Er stand beim (or am or neben dem) Fenster	He was standing by the window

(b) It is used like the French *chez* for *at the house of* [for *to the house of*, zu is used; see paragraph **268 (a)**]:

Er wohnt bei seinen Eltern	He lives with his parents

(c) It means *with* or *among*, referring to nations or communities:

Bei den Juden, Franzosen	Among the Jews, French

(d) It means *with* or *on*, referring to persons:

Ich habe kein Geld (Buch) bei mir	I have no money (book) on me (or with me)

(e) Referring to battles, it means *of* or *near*:

Die Schlacht bei Leipzig	The battle of Leipzig

(f) Other phrases:

Beim Frühstück, Mittagessen usw.	At breakfast, lunch, etc.
Bei Tisch	At table
Bei diesem Wetter	In this weather
Bei diesen Worten	At these words
Bei dieser Gelegenheit	At this opportunity, on this occasion
Bei der Arbeit	At work
Bei seiner Ankunft	On his arrival
Beim Lesen des Briefes	On or while reading the letter
Bei der Hand fassen	To take by the hand

260. Mit.

(a) Mit generally means *with*. [For its use with the passive, see paragraph **249 (c)**]. It is often used without a pronoun:

Kommen Sie mit?	Are you coming (with me, with us)?

(b) It means *by*, referring to means of transport:

Mit dem Zug, Dampfer, Auto, (Fahr)rad	By train, steamer, car, bicycle

(c) Other phrases:

Mit der Zeit	In (the course of) time
Mit Recht, mit Unrecht	Rightly, wrongly
Ich redete mit ihm	I was talking to him
Mit den Zähnen knirschen	To gnash the teeth
Mit dem Schwanz wedeln	To wag the tail

261. Nach nearly always precedes the word that it governs, except when used as in section **(c)**.

(a) Nach means *to*, with proper names of places:

Nach Berlin, nach Deutschland	To Berlin, to Germany

(b) It also means *after*:

Nach einer Weile	After a while
Einer nach dem andern	One after the other

(c) When it means *according to*, it sometimes follows the word that it governs:

Nach seinem Brief ist er krank	According to his letter, he is ill
Nach meiner Meinung (or meiner Meinung nach)	In my opinion
Nach Belieben	As desired

(d) Other phrases:

Nach Hause gehen (or fahren)	To go home
Nach oben, nach außen usw.	Upwards, outwards, etc.
Nach dem Meter, Pfund usw. verkaufen	To sell by the yard, pound, etc.
Je nach den Umständen	According to the circumstances

(e) For the difference between nach, nachdem, and nachher, see paragraph **330**.

262. Seit.

(a) Seit generally means *since*:

Seit seiner Ankunft   Since his arrival

(b) For the use of present or imperfect with seit, instead of the English perfect or pluperfect, see paragraph **441 (c)**.

(c) For the difference between seit, seitdem, and seither, see paragraph **333**.

263. Von.

(a) Von is sometimes used to translate *of*. For choosing between von and the genitive to translate *of*, see next three paragraphs.

(b) It often means *about* (*on the subject of*):

Wir sprechen, schreiben von   We are talking, writing about
den Ferien   the holidays

(c) It often means *from*:

Von Jahr zu Jahr, von Ort   From year to year, from
zu Ort   place to place
Ich habe von ihm gehört[1]   I have heard from him

(d) It is used with the passive for *by* [see paragraph **249 (a)**]:

Der Brief wurde von ihm   The letter was written by
geschrieben   him

264. Von or the genitive. It is not always easy to know whether to translate *of* by the genitive or by von. The genitive is generally better:

Der Preis des Buches   The price of the book
Die Dauer des Krieges   The duration of the war
Der älteste dieser Männer   The oldest of these men
Der Tod eines Freundes   The death of a friend
Ein Teil des Hauses   Part of the house
Ein Ausruf des Schreckens   An exclamation of terror

[1] Von ihm might mean here either *from* or *about him*; *about him* should therefore be translated über ihn.

265. Von is used instead of the genitive in the following constructions:

(a) When *of* means *about* or *concerning* [unless über is used, as in paragraph **281 (c)**]:

Wir sprechen von ihm (or über ihn)	We are talking of (or about) him

(b) In titles:

Der Herzog von Braunschweig	The Duke of Brunswick

(c) When the genitive has no special ending to distinguish it:

Die Schüler von heute	The schoolboys of today
Der Preis von sechs Büchern	The price of six books

(d) Before pronouns standing alone:

Jeder von uns[1]	Each of us

266. 'Of' not translated. The German construction omits *of*, and puts the two nouns in apposition, both taking the same case:

(a) In most expressions of measurement [see paragraph **197 (a)**].

This construction is also often used with such nouns as die Anzahl, *number*; die Masse, *mass*; die Menge, *quantity, crowd*, if the following noun stands alone. If it does not stand alone, it is usually in the genitive:

Eine große Menge Menschen	A great crowd of people
Eine große Menge aufgeregter Menschen	A great crowd of excited people

(b) After voll(er), *full of*. Voller is generally used if the following noun stands alone: otherwise voll is preferred and the noun is usually in the genitive:

Der Platz war voll(er) Menschen	The square was full of people
Der Platz war voll lärmender Menschen	The square was full of noisy people

---

[1] The genitive would have to be used after a verb taking the genitive: Er gedenkt unser, *He thinks of us*.

(c) Generally when the second noun can be logically regarded as being in apposition to the first, without the existence of any special relation (such as possession) between them:

Die Stadt London	The town of London
Die Firma Schmidt	The firm of Smith
Der Monat Januar	The month of January
Das Königreich England[1]	The kingdom of England

267. Other ways of expressing 'of':

(a) By a compound noun:

Die Eintrittskarte	Ticket of admission
Die Geistesgegenwart	Presence of mind

(b) By an adjective:

Die dortigen Sitten	The customs of that place
Ein vermögender Mann	A man of property

268. Zu.

(a) Zu means *to*, referring to persons:

Kommen Sie her zu mir[2]	Come here to me
Er geht zum Buchhändler	He is going to the book-seller's

(b) It is used before an indirect object if direct speech is being quoted:

Er sagte zu mir: „Ich kann nicht kommen"	He said to me, " I cannot come "

(c) It is generally used for *to*, referring to places, if proper names are not used [see also auf, paragraph 275 (c), and in, paragraph 278 (b)]:

Der Weg zum Bahnhof, zum Rathaus	The way to the station, to the town-hall

---

[1] *The rivers of England* would be die Flüsse Englands, as possession is implied.

[2] If the word in the dative is an indirect object, zu is not used: Er gab dem Jungen das Buch, *He gave the boy the book.*

(d) It is sometimes used for *at*, referring to towns and villages; though in is more often used in conversation:

Er ift zu (or in) Kiel geboren	He was born at Kiel
Er wohnt in Kiel	He lives at Kiel

(e) It is used for *at* or *in*, referring to seasons and times [for the time of day, however, um is used; see paragraph **190 (a)**]:

Zu Oftern, zu Weihnachten	At Easter, at Christmas
Zur Zeit Karls des Großen	In the time of Charlemagne

(f) It means *at*, referring to prices:

Fleifch zu einer Mark das Pfund	Meat at a shilling a pound

(g) It means *for*, referring to purpose:

Zu diefem Zweck	For that purpose
Zum Beften der Kranken	For the (benefit of the) sick
Zum Beifpiel	For example
Zum Spaß	For a joke
Zum Bergnügen	For pleasure

(h) Other phrases:

Zu Fuß, zu Pferd	On foot, on horseback
Zu Waffer, zu Lande	By water, by land
Zum zweiten, dritten Male	For the second, third time
Tee, Kaffee zum Frühftück	Tea, coffee for breakfast
Zu Boden fallen	To fall to the ground
Zu feinem Berdruß	To his annoyance
Zu Ende	At an end, over
Zum Schluß	In conclusion
Zur Not	In case of need

269. Other prepositions governing the dative. The prepositions given in paragraph **256 (b)** are less often used, but the following need special notice:

(a) Binnen may govern either the genitive or the dative. As a preposition it is used only in expressions of time, though in compounds such as das Binnenland, *inland country*, it refers to place.

(b) Entgegen follows the word that it governs. It is generally used as a separable prefix.

(c) Gemäß generally follows the word that it governs.

(d) Längs may govern either the genitive or the dative.

(e) Ob means *beyond* and governs the dative, or means *because of* and governs the genitive.

(f) Zufolge generally governs the dative, which it follows. Occasionally it governs the genitive, which it precedes.

(g) Zuwider follows the word that it governs.

PREPOSITIONS GOVERNING THE DATIVE OR ACCUSATIVE

270. The following prepositions govern the dative or accusative :

an, by, on, at, to	in, in, into	unter, under
auf, on	neben, beside, near	vor, in front of, before
hinter, behind	über, over, above	zwischen, between

271. These prepositions refer mainly to place. The general rule as to the case to be used is: if the sentence answers the question "where?" use the dative; if it answers the question "whither?" use the accusative:

Das Buch liegt auf dem Pult	The book is on the desk
Er legt das Buch auf das Pult	He puts the book on the desk
Er lief vor ihm	He ran before him (all the time)
Er lief vor ihn	He ran in front of him (from some other position)
Er ging auf der Straße	He was walking in the street
Er ging auf die Straße	He walked into the street
Der Tunnel liegt unter der Elbe	The tunnel is under the Elbe
Der Tunnel führt unter die Elbe	The tunnel leads under the Elbe

272. An with the dative.

(a) Meaning *at, near, against, by the side of*:

Er ſaß an ſeinem Pult	He was sitting at his desk
Das Bild hing an der Wand	The picture hung on the wall
Er ſtand am Fenſter, an ſeiner Seite	He was standing by the window, at his side

(b) Referring to time [see paragraph **191** (c)]:

Am Morgen	In the morning
Am 1. Juni	On the 1st June

(c) Other phrases:

Die Stadt liegt am Fluß, an der See	The town is on the river, on the sea
Er ging am Hauſe vorbei	He walked past the house
Am Ufer	On the shore
Am Himmel	In the sky
Am Ende	In the end, in the long run
An ſeiner Stelle	In his place
An Bord	On board

273. An with the accusative, meaning *at* or *to*:

Er ſetzte ſich an ſein Pult	He sat down at his desk
Er hängte das Bild an die Wand	He hung the picture on the wall
Er ging ans Fenſter	He went to the window
Wir fahren an die See	We are going to the sea

274. Auf with the dative.

(a) Meaning *on* (*top of*):

Das Buch liegt auf dem Pult	The book is on the desk

(b) It is often used to mean *in* or *at*, referring to streets, buildings, and open places:

Auf der Straße, auf dem Markt, Platz, Gang, Felde, Lande	In the street, at the market, in the square, corridor, field, country

(c) Other phrases:

Auf der Stelle	On the spot (at once)
Auf dem Weg sein	To be on the way
Auf der Jagd sein	To be hunting
Auf dem Posten sein	To be at one's post
Auf der Lauer sein	To be on the watch
Auf seiner Seite sein	To be on his side

275. Auf with the accusative.

(a) Meaning *on* (*top of*):

Er legt das Buch auf das Pult   He puts the book on the
                                 desk

(b) Meaning *for*, referring to future time [see paragraph
192 (d)]:

Er reist auf drei Monate nach   He is going to Berlin for
  Berlin   three months

(c) Other phrases:

Aufs Land fahren	To go into the country
Auf die Jagd gehen	To go hunting
Auf diese Weise	In this way
Auf Befragen	On request
Auf seinen Wunsch	At his wish
Auf eigne Faust	Off (his) own bat
Schlag auf Schlag	Blow after blow

276. Hinter means *behind*:

Er stand hinter der Tür	He stood behind the door
Er ging hinter die Tür	He went behind the door

277. In with the dative.

(a) Meaning *in*, referring to time or place:

In einem Jahre	In a year
Das Buch ist im Pult	The book is in the desk

(b) Other phrases:

Im Alter von	At the age of
In der Schule, in der Kirche, im Konzert	At school, at church, at the concert

In der Schlacht bei Leipzig	At the battle of Leipzig
Im ersten Stock	On the first floor
Im Himmel	In heaven
In diesem Augenblick	At that moment
Im großen und ganzen	On the whole
Im Gegenteil	On the contrary
Im Begriff sein, zu . . .	To be about to . . .
Im Auftrage von	On behalf of
In dieser Absicht	For that purpose
Im Stich lassen	To leave in the lurch
Heute in acht (vierzehn) Tagen	Today week (fortnight)

278. In with the accusative.

() Meaning *into*:

Er steckte das Buch ins Pult	He put the book into the desk

(b) Other phrases:

In die Schule, in die Kirche, in die Stadt, ins Theater gehen	To go to school, to church, to town, to the theatre
Er hat sich in den Finger geschnitten	He has cut his finger
In Frage kommen	To come in question
In die Ferien gehen	To go on one's holidays

279. Neben means *beside, by, at the side of*:

Er stand neben der Tür	He stood by the door
Er setzte sich neben die Tür	He sat down by the door

280. Über with the dative means *over* or *above*:

Es liegen Wolken über den Bergen	There are clouds over the hills

281. Über with the accusative.

() Meaning *over* or *across*:

Er schwamm über (or durch) den Fluß	He swam across the river

(b) Meaning *over (more than)*:

Das Paket wiegt über ein Pfund	The parcel weighs over a pound

(c) Meaning *about (concerning)*:

Wir sprachen viel über das Ereignis	We talked a great deal about the occurrence

(d) Meaning *via*:

Der Zug fährt über Berlin	The train goes via Berlin

(e) Other phrases:

Heute über acht (vierzehn) Tage	Today week (fortnight)
Über alles Maß	Beyond measure
Über die Gebühr	To excess
Über kurz oder lang	Sooner or later

282. Unter with the dative.

(a) Meaning *under, among, amid*:

Das Buch lag unter dem Pult	The book was under the desk
Unter Freunden geschieht das nicht	That does not happen among friends
Unter allgemeinem Gelächter	Amid general laughter

(b) Meaning *under (less than)*:[1]

Das Paket wiegt unter einem Pfund	The parcel weighs under a pound

(c) Other phrases:

Unter seiner Regierung	In his reign
Unter dieser Bedingung	On that condition
Unter diesem Vorwand	On that pretext
Unter diesen Umständen	In (or under) those circumstances

283. Unter with the accusative means *under, among*:

Er ließ das Buch unter das Pult fallen	He dropped the book under the desk
Er geht unter seine Freunde	He is going among his friends

[1] Contrast über with the accusative [paragraph 281 (b)].

284. Vor with the dative.

(a) Meaning *before* (referring to time or place), *in front of*:

Vor dem Kriege	Before the war
Er stand vor der Tür	He stood in front of the door

(b) Meaning *ago* [see paragraph **191 (c)**]:

Das ist vor zwei Tagen, vor langer Zeit, vor kurzem geschehen	That happened two days ago, a long time ago, a short time ago

(c) Meaning *with* or *for*, referring to mental or physical feelings:

Er tanzte vor Freude	He danced for joy
Er zitterte vor Kälte	He shivered with cold

(d) For the difference between vor, bevor, and vorher, see paragraph **323**.

285. Vor with the accusative means *before, in front of*:

Er stellte sich vor die Tür	He placed himself in front of the door

286. Zwischen means *between*:

Er stand zwischen ihnen	He stood between them
Er stellte sich zwischen sie	He placed himself between them

PREPOSITIONS GOVERNING THE GENITIVE

287. The following prepositions govern the genitive:

(a) The following are those most commonly used:

außerhalb, outside
innerhalb, inside
oberhalb, above
unterhalb, below
diesseit(s), on this side of
jenseit(s), on that side of
(an)statt, instead of

*trotz, in spite of
um . . . willen, for the sake of
während, during
†wegen, because of, on account of

(b) The following adverbs of place have come to be used as prepositions:

links, to the left of	östlich, to the east of
rechts, to the right of	westlich, to the west of
nördlich, to the north of	unfern ⎫
südlich, to the south of	unweit ⎭ not far from

(c) The following are less used, and can often be replaced by shorter prepositions:

... halb ⎫	einschließlich, including
... halben ⎬ on account of	infolge, in consequence of
halber ⎭	inmitten, in the middle of
mittels[1] ⎫ by means of	kraft ⎫ by virtue of
vermittels[1] ⎭	vermöge ⎭
anläßlich, on the occasion of	laut, in accordance with
behufs ⎫ for the purpose of	mangels, for want of
zwecks ⎭	ob, because of
bezüglich ⎫ regarding	seitens, on the part of
hinsichtlich ⎭	ungeachtet, notwithstanding

288. Notes on these prepositions.

(a) Anstatt and statt mean the same, and it is not necessary to use the longer form.

(b) Diesseit(s) and jenseit(s) must take the final =s when used as adverbs, but need not do so as prepositions.

(c) ... halb and ... halben are used only in compounds, such as deshalb, *therefore*; meinethalb, *on my account, for my sake*. Halber is used in compounds and also as a separate word, and it follows the word that it governs.

(d) Ob. See paragraph **269** (e).

(e) Trotz may govern the genitive or, less often, the dative. It forms the adverb trotzdem, *nevertheless, for all that.*

---

[1] Sometimes the forms mittelst and vermittelst are used.

(f) Um . . . willen forms such phrases as um meinet⸗willen, *for my sake, on my account, for all I care*; um seines Vaters willen, *for his father's sake*, etc.

(g) Ungeachtet forms the adverb dessenungeachtet, *nevertheless*. When used as a separate word, it precedes the word that it governs.

(h) Wegen usually precedes, but may follow, the word that it governs. It forms compounds in the same way as . . . halb and . . . willen, such as meinetwegen, *on my account, for all I care*, etc. The use of the dative with wegen is a provincialism, and should be avoided.

USE OF PREPOSITIONS WITH VERBS, NOUNS, AND ADJECTIVES

289. The prepositions used in German and English phrases do not always correspond to the meanings given in the preceding paragraphs; for instance, *to strive for* is streben nach, *proud of* is stolz auf, and so on. The following paragraphs give some guide to the use of German prepositions with verbs, nouns, and adjectives.

290. An with the dative.

(a)

arbeiten an, to work on or at
s. (er)freuen an, to enjoy
erkennen an, to recognise by
fassen an (or bei), to seize by
fehlen an,[1] to lack
gleichen an, to resemble in
leiden an, to suffer from
s. rächen an, to take revenge on

riechen an, to smell (at)
sterben an, to die of
teilnehmen an, to take part in
übertreffen an, to surpass in
verhindern an, to prevent from
verzweifeln an, to despair of
ziehen an, to pull at or by
zweifeln an, to doubt

Er hat am Gewinn teil⸗genommen

He has shared in the profit(s)

Ich erkannte ihn an seiner Stimme

I recognised him by his voice

[1] Impersonal.

(b)

der Anteil an, share in
die Abnahme an, decrease in
die Zunahme an, increase in
die Freude an
das Vergnügen an } pleasure in

der Geschmack an, taste for
der Mangel an, lack of
die Not an, need of
der Zweifel an, doubt of

Ein Mangel an Rohstoffen

A lack of raw materials

(c)

ähnlich an
gleich an } similar in
arm an, poor in

krank an, ill of or with
reich an, rich in

Er ist krank am Fieber

He is ill with fever

291. An with the accusative.

(a)

denken an, to think of
erinnern an, to remind of
gewöhnen an, to accustom to
glauben an, to believe in
s. lehnen an, to lean against

richten an, to address to
schreiben an,[1] to write to
s. wenden an, to turn or apply to
zahlen an,[1] to pay to

Er erinnerte mich an die Sache
Wir denken an die Zukunft
Er lehnte sich an den Tisch
Ich habe einen Brief an ihn (or ihm einen Brief) geschrieben

He reminded me of the matter
We think of the future
He leaned on the table
I have written him a letter

Denken an (French *penser à*) means *to have in mind*; denken von (French *penser de*) means *to have an opinion about*; viel halten von means *to have a high opinion of*:

Ich denke an die Ferien
Was (or wie) denken Sie davon?
Ich halte viel von ihm

I am thinking of the holidays
What do you think of it?
I think very highly of him

[1] The dative (indirect object) may be used instead of an, as in the fourth example.

(b)

das Andenken, die Erinnerung an, memory of
die Bitte an, request to
im Anschluß an, referring to, in connection with

Im Anschluß an Ihren Brief
Er richtete (or stellte) die Frage an den Jungen

eine Frage richten (or stellen) an, to ask . . . a question
der Gedanke an, thought of
der Glaube an, belief in
der Gruß an, greeting to

Referring to your letter
He asked the boy the question

292. Auf with the dative.

spielen auf (der Geige usw.), to play on (the violin, etc.)
beruhen auf, to rest on

beharren auf (or bei or in), to persist in
bestehen auf, to insist on

Spielen may be used transitively: Er spielt Klavier, Geige, *He plays the piano, violin*; and bestehen auf may be followed by the accusative.

293. Auf generally takes the accusative. The following are common examples:

(a)

achten auf, to heed
anspielen auf, to allude to
antworten auf, to answer (a question, etc.)
beschränken auf, to limit to
beziehen auf, to refer to
blicken auf, to look at
(ein)wirken auf, to influence
s. freuen auf, to look forward to
gründen auf, to base or found on
hinweisen auf, to point out, indicate
hoffen auf, to hope for
hören auf, to listen (pay heed) to
rechnen auf, to count on

schätzen auf, to value or estimate at
schießen auf, to shoot at
steuern auf, to steer towards
s. stürzen auf, to rush up to
s. stützen auf, to support oneself on
s. verlassen auf
vertrauen auf } to rely on
verschieben auf, to postpone till
verzichten auf, to renounce
vorbereiten auf, to prepare for
warten auf, to wait for
zielen auf, to aim at
zugehen auf, to go up to
zukommen auf, to come up to

Antworten Sie mir auf meine Frage[1]	Answer (me) my question
Wir freuen uns auf die Ferien	We are looking forward to the holidays
Er kam auf mich zu	He came up to me

(b)

achtsam auf, heedful of	gefaßt auf, prepared or ready for
aufmerksam auf, attentive to	
bedacht auf, intent on	neidisch auf, envious of
böse auf, angry with	stolz auf, proud of
Er ist stolz auf seinen Hund	He is proud of his dog

294. Aus.

bestehen aus, to consist of	s. ergeben aus, to result from
entstehen aus, to arise from	schließen aus, to infer from
ersehen aus, to see (perceive) from	werden aus, to become of
Das besteht aus zwei Teilen	That consists of two parts
Was ist aus ihr geworden?	What has become of her?

295. Für.

halten für, to consider	schwärmen für, to be enthusiastic about
s. interessieren für, to interest oneself in	
	Der Beweis für, proof of
Ich halte ihn für einen Schuft	I consider him a rascal

296. Gegen is a good deal used of sentiments, both friendly and unfriendly; but its use is not confined to such words:

argwöhnisch gegen ⎫ suspicious of	die Abneigung gegen, disinclination for
mißtrauisch gegen ⎭	
gütig, freundlich gegen, kind, pleasant to(wards)	der Einwand gegen, objection to
empfindlich gegen, sensitive to	die Treue gegen, fidelity to(wards)
wirksam gegen, effective, efficacious against	die Verachtung gegen, contempt for

[1] Or Beantworten Sie mir meine Frage.

sicher gegen, safe against

der Widerwille gegen, repugnance for

Er ist sicher gegen jeden An=
griff (or vor jedem Angriff)

He is safe against all attacks

297. In with the dative.

ankommen in[1] ⎫ to arrive at
anlangen in[1] ⎭ or reach
bestehen in, to consist in

geschickt in ⎫ clever at
gewandt in ⎭

Wir kamen in der Stadt an

We arrived at the town

Er ist sehr geschickt im Zeichnen

He is very clever at drawing

298. In with the accusative.

s. einmengen in ⎫ to interfere
s. einmischen in ⎭ or meddle with

verwickeln in, to involve in
(ver)hüllen in, to wrap in
kleiden in, to dress in
verliebt in, in love with
die Einsicht in, insight into

einwilligen in, to consent to
gelangen in, to arrive in, reach
s. schicken in, to accommodate
oneself to

Er willigte in den Vorschlag
ein

He consented to the proposal

Sie hüllte sich in einen Mantel

She wrapped herself in a cloak

299. Mit.

s. abfinden mit, to accommodate oneself or settle
down to

drohen mit, to threaten with
handeln mit, to deal in
prahlen mit, to boast of
verwechseln mit, to mistake
for, confuse with

aufhören mit, to stop or have
done with

300. Nach is very much used with verbs denoting effort, such as *to send for, search for, grasp at*:

fragen nach, to ask (about)
s. erkundigen nach, to inquire
about

forschen nach, to inquire into
greifen nach, to grasp at
riechen nach, to smell of

---

[1] Similarly with other prepositions such as an and auf: Wir kamen auf
dem Bahnhof an, *We arrived at the station.*

ſchicken nach, to send for
ſ. ſehnen nach, to long for
ſtreben nach ⎱ to strive for
trachten nach ⎰

ſchmecken nach, to taste of
ſuchen nach, to search for
urteilen nach, to judge by

Wir ſchickten nach dem Arzt
Er urteilt nach dem Schein
Ich fragte ihn nach ſeinem
    Alter

We sent for the doctor
He judges by appearances
I asked him his age

301. Über, when used figuratively, takes the accusative:

(a)

ſ. ärgern über, to be vexed at
ſ. beſchweren über, bei, to
    make a complaint about, to
ſ. freuen über, to be pleased at
klagen über, to complain of
lachen über, to laugh at
murren über, to grumble at

nachdenken über, to reflect on
ſpotten über, to mock (at)
ſprechen über, to speak about
tröſten über, to console for
verfügen über, to control,
    dispose of
wundern über, to wonder at

Wir lachten (freuten uns) ſehr
    über ſeinen Brief

We laughed very much at
(were very pleased about)
    his letter

Er beſchwerte ſich beim Vor=
    ſteher darüber

He complained about it to
    the manager

(b)

der Aufſatz über, essay on
die Bemerkung über, obser-
    vation on
die Freude über, joy at
das Geſpräch über, conversa-
    tion about

der Zweifel über, doubt about
betrübt über, depressed at
empört über, indignant at
erſtaunt über, astonished at
zornig über, angry at

Er war erſtaunt über das
    Ereignis

He was astonished at the
    occurrence

302. Um often means *for*, after verbs such as **bitten**,
kämpfen, or **ſpielen**, when something is wished for or is in

dispute [for its use after such words as größer, länger, höher, etc., see paragraph 253 (c)]:

(a)

ſ. bemühen um, to take pains over	kämpfen um, to fight for
beneiden um, to envy (for)	kommen um, to lose
ſ. bewerben um, to apply for	ſ. kümmern um, to bother about
betrügen um, to defraud of	ringen um, to wrestle or struggle for
bitten um, to ask for	
bringen um, to deprive of	ſpielen um, to play for
flehen um, to plead for	ſtreiten um, to quarrel about
ſ. handeln um,[1] to be a question of	trauern um, to mourn for

Er bat mich um mein Fahrrad	He asked me for my bicycle
Es handelt ſich um ſeine Ehre	It is a question of his honour
Man brachte ihn um ſein Leben	He was killed (deliberately)
Er kam um ſein Leben	He lost his life

(b)

die Bitte um, request for	beſorgt um, anxious about
der Kummer um, concern for	verlegen um, perplexed about, at a loss for
die Sorge um, anxiety about	

Der Kampf um die Freiheit	The struggle for freedom

303. Von.

abhängen von, to depend on	leben von, to live on
benachrichtigen von (or über with acc.), to inform of	ſ. nähren von, to feed on
	ſprechen von, to speak of
freiſprechen von ⎫ to acquit losſprechen von ⎬ of	überzeugen von, to convince of
heilen von, to cure of	wimmeln von, to swarm with

Wir ſprachen viel davon (or darüber)	We talked a great deal about it
Das hängt vom Wetter ab	That depends on the weather

[1] Impersonal.

304. Vor, when used figuratively, takes the dative. Sich hüten vor, like the French *se garder de,* means *to take care not to*:

ſ. fürchten vor, to be afraid of	die Achtung vor, respect for
ſ. grauen vor, to dread	der Ekel vor, disgust at
ſ. hüten vor, to beware of	die Furcht vor, fear of
retten vor, to save from	
fliehen vor, to flee from	
ſchützen vor (or gegen or wider), to protect from or against	
warnen vor, to warn of or against	

Ich werde mich davor hüten	I shall take care not to do it
Er fürchtete ſich vor der Gefahr	He was afraid of the danger

305. Zu.

(a)

auffordern zu, to summon to	(ein)laden zu, to invite to
beglückwünſchen zu } to congratulate on gratulieren zu	gebrauchen zu, to use for
	gehören zu,[1] to belong to
	machen zu, to make
berechtigen zu, to entitle to	werden zu, to become
dienen zu, to serve or be used for	zwingen zu, to compel to

Er machte ihn zu ſeinem Freund	He made him his friend
Der Junge iſt zum Mann (or ein Mann) geworden	The boy has become a man
Ein Meſſer dient zum Schneiden	A knife is used (serves) for cutting

(b) Verbs like machen, *to make*; ernennen, *to appoint*; erwählen, *to elect,* are used transitively in the ordinary way: Sie (er)wählten einen Kapitän, *They elected a captain*;

---

[1] Used with zu, gehören implies membership; with the dative only, it implies ownership:

Er gehört zu keiner Partei	He does not belong to any party
Das Haus gehört meinem Vater	The house belongs to my father

but the object may be followed by zum or zur and a noun, representing the complement of the object:

Sie (er)wählten ihn zum Kapitän	They elected him captain

(c)

der Anlaß zu, occasion of	bereit zu,[1] ready for
der Grund zu, reason for	geeignet zu,[1] suitable for
die Gelegenheit zu, opportunity for	nötig zu,[1] necessary for
	tauglich zu,[1] fit or appropriate for
die Liebe zu, love for	
die Neigung zu, inclination or affection for	verpflichtet zu,[1] obliged or bound to

Der Anlaß zum Streit war unklar	The occasion of the quarrel was not clear
Ich fühlte mich zum Schweigen verpflichtet	I felt obliged to say nothing
Das ist nötig zur Reise	That is necessary for the journey

306. Prepositions followed by verbs. Only three prepositions may govern a verb; they are (an)statt, *instead of*; ohne, *without*; and um, *in order to*. They all take an infinitive with zu, and the phrase must be separated from the rest of the sentence by a comma:

(An)statt sein Buch zu lesen	Instead of reading his book
Ohne sein Buch zu lesen	Without reading his book
Um sein Buch zu lesen	In order to read his book

307. English prepositions followed by verbs. For the translation of the English preposition and gerund, in such phrases as *on his hearing that, in doing so, the fact of his being here*, etc., see paragraph **416** (c).

---

[1] In this construction. the noun that follows refers to things, not to persons.

IX

CONJUNCTIONS

CO-ORDINATING CONJUNCTIONS

308. The following six conjunctions introduce co-ordinate clauses, and do not affect the order of words:

aber, but, however	**oder,** or
allein, but, only	**sondern,** but
denn, for	**und,** and

Doch, *but, yet,* is sometimes used as a co-ordinating conjunction, as in paragraph **214 (d).**

All these conjunctions, except **aber,** must come at the beginning of the clause.

309. Aber is used in four different positions in the clause:

(a) At the beginning of the clause:

Meine Mutter ist hier, aber mein Vater kommt nicht — My mother is here, but my father is not coming

(b) After the subject (without a comma):

Sein Begleiter aber stand auf — But his companion stood up (or His companion, however, etc.)

(c) After the verb (without a comma):

Das ist aber ganz falsch — But that is quite wrong (or That is quite wrong, however)

(d) Sometimes, when the subject of the two co-ordinate clauses is the same, it is omitted in the second clause, and **aber** is put after the verb. This construction is not usual in conversation:

Er ſuchte ſeinen Freund den ganzen Morgen, konnte ihn aber nicht finden (konnte aber keine Spur von ihm finden) | He looked for his friend all morning, but could not find him (but could not find any trace of him)

310. Allein.

(a) Allein is not used as much as aber. The English use *only* in much the same way (unemphasised):

Es blies heftig, aber (or allein) es regnete nicht | It was blowing hard, but (or only) it was not raining

(b) Allein is also an adverb meaning *alone*:

Er iſt allein gekommen | He has come alone

311. Translation of 'only.' *Only* may be (a) an adjective, (b) and (c) an adverb, or (d) a conjunction:

(a) Johann iſt ſein einziges Kind | John is his only child

(b) Er hat nur ein Kind | He has only one child

(c) Er iſt erſt zehn Jahre alt | He is only ten years old[1]

(d) Allein (or aber) es regnete nicht | Only (or but) it was not raining

312. Denn.

(a) When used as a conjunction, denn begins the clause; used as an adverb [see paragraph **213** (b)], it does not:

Ich weiß nicht, was er ſagt, denn ich kann ihn nicht hören | I don't know what he is saying, for I can't hear him
Wie kommt das denn? | Why, how is that?

(b) For the difference between denn and für, see paragraph **251** (b).

313. Sondern. For the difference between ſondern and aber, see paragraph **238**.

[1] See paragraph **217**.

314. Und is generally used as in English. The following points should be noticed:

(a) Und is not generally used to separate two adjectives before a noun:

Eine schnelle, unerwartete Be= wegung	A quick and unexpected movement

(b) Und is generally used with a finite verb in such expressions as *to be so kind as to* . . . or *to be good enough to* . . . :

Er war so gut und beantwor= tete mir meinen Brief um= gehend.	He was kind enough to answer my letter by return

(c) Und is not used in such expressions as *nice and warm* (schön warm).

(d) The expression und zwar need not always be translated. It is preceded by a comma:

Die Dampfer fahren zweimal wöchentlich, und zwar mitt= wochs und sonnabends	The steamers sail twice a week, on Wednesdays and Saturdays

(e) If und begins a clause needing the inverted order, the subject must not be omitted, but must be represented, if necessary, by a personal pronoun:

Er blieb einen Augenblick stehen, und dann ging er ins Haus	He stopped a moment, and then went into the house

315. Punctuation with und. When two co-ordinate clauses joined by und have the same subject, which is not expressed in the second clause, they are not separated by a comma [see also paragraphs **61** and **173** on commas between nouns and adjectives respectively]:

Zuletzt stand das junge Mädchen auf und gab dem Jungen verstohlen einen Wink, und beide setzten sich im Hinter= grunde der Stube auf das Sofa, stellten ein Spiel zwischen sich und spielten eifrig.

316. Order of words. If und, aber, oder, or sondern connects two subordinate clauses, the transposed order must, of course, be used:

Als er hinausschaute und den Regen bemerkte	When he looked out and noticed the rain

SUBORDINATING CONJUNCTIONS

317. The following conjunctions introduce subordinate clauses. Those in paragraph (**b**) are less common than those in paragraph (**a**).

(a)

als, as, than, when
als ob ⎫
als wenn ⎬ as if
bevor ⎫
ehe ⎬ before
bis, till, until
da, as, since
damit, in order that
damit nicht, lest
daß, that
falls, in case
indem ⎫
während ⎬ while

nachdem, after
ob, whether
obgleich, although
seit, seitdem, since
so . . . (used with adverb), as . . . as
weil, because
wenn, if, when
wenn auch, though, although
wenn nicht, unless
wie, as
[See also paragraph **341**]

(b)

indessen ⎫
unterdessen ⎬ while

obschon ⎫
obwohl ⎪
wenngleich ⎬ though, although
wennschon ⎪
wiewohl ⎭

318. Punctuation. In using these conjunctions, it is important to remember that a subordinate clause is always separated from the main clause by a comma:

Warten Sie, bis ich komme	Wait till I come
Fragen Sie ihn, ob er es weiß	Ask him whether he knows it

319. Order of words.

(a) As these conjunctions introduce subordinate clauses, the verb used with them must come at the end of the clause, the auxiliary, if any, being last of all [see paragraph **471**]:

Als ich ihn sah	When I saw him
Nachdem ich ihn gesehen hatte	After I had seen him

(b) A main clause takes the inverted order when it is preceded by a clause that is subordinate to it:

Da er gekommen ist, darf er bleiben	As he has come, he may stay
Als er ankam, war er müde	When he arrived, he was tired

(c) The rule given in section (b) is sometimes ignored after an adverb clause of concession; but more often the main clause begins with **doch**, and is inverted:

Wenn es auch schwer ist, wir müssen es doch tun (or doch müssen wir es tun)	Although it is difficult, we must do it

(d) The subject is usually put immediately after the subordinating conjunction, though it may be put later for emphasis:

Als er nach mehreren Versuchen die Tür aufmachte	When, after several attempts, he opened the door
Als einige Minuten später der Präsident erschien	When, a few minutes later, the president appeared

320. Als.

(a) For the difference between **als, wann,** and **wenn,** see paragraph **193**.

(b) **Als** is used with the historical present, as well as with the past, meaning *as* or *when*:

Und als er auf seinem stattlichen Roß	And as he came[1] riding, etc.
In eine Au kommt geritten	

[1] See paragraph **441** (b).

(c) For the use of als and wie in comparisons of adjectives and adverbs, see paragraphs **165** and **207**.

(d) Als (*as*) and wie (*like*) are used in the following constructions, als denoting identity, and wie denoting similarity:

Er sprach als Freund	He spoke as a friend
Er sprach wie ein Freund	He spoke like a friend

In the second of the above examples, wie, a conjunction, is translated by *like*, a preposition. The sentence means literally *He spoke as a friend* (*would speak*).

(e) Words in apposition, connected by als, are in the same case:

Er sprach als mein Freund	He spoke as my friend
Ich erkannte ihn als meinen Freund	I recognised him as my friend

321. Als ob and als wenn. The ob or wenn may be omitted, and the inverted order used [as in paragraph **337(b)**]:

Er ging langsam, als wäre er müde (or als ob or als wenn er müde wäre)	He was walking slowly, as if he were tired

322. Bevor and ehe. Ehe is the more commonly used in conversation.

323. Translation of 'before.' Vor (preposition) and ehe and bevor (conjunctions) mean *before*, and vorher (adverb) means *before*(*hand*) or *previously*:

Vor Weihnachten	Before Christmas
Ehe (or bevor) er kam	Before he came
Ich hatte ihn schon vorher gesehen	I had seen him before(hand)

324. Bis. In translating *not till*, it is often better to avoid bis and use erst [see also paragraphs **217** and **248**]:

Ich erkannte ihn erst, als ich seinen Namen hörte	I did not recognise him till I heard his name

325. Da.

(a) For the use of ba as adverb and as conjunction, see paragraph **212**.

(b) Da and ſeit both mean *since*, but ba refers to reason, and ſeit to time:

Da er gekommen iſt	Since (as) he has come
Seit(dem) er gekommen iſt	(During the time) since he has come

326. Damit means *in order that*, or *so that*, implying purpose (*so that*, implying result, is baß or ſo baß—see paragraph **327 (c)**]:

Ich gab ihm den Schlüſſel, damit er die Tür zuſchließen konnte	I gave him the key, so that he could lock the door

327. Daß.

(a) For the use of the subjunctive or indicative after baß, see paragraphs **430** ff.

(b) Daß is very often omitted in German, just as the conjunction *that* is very often omitted in English. When this happens, the verb takes the normal order, instead of being put last:

Ich weiß gewiß, er iſt krank (or daß er krank iſt)	I know for certain he is ill (or that he is ill)

(c) Daß is used in als baß, auf baß, ohne baß, and ſo baß. Auf baß means the same as damit (see previous paragraph). The following sentences illustrate als baß, ohne baß, and ſo baß:

Er iſt zu krank, als daß ich ihn verlaſſen könnte	He is too ill for me to leave him
Das Auto wurde zertrümmert, ohne daß er verletzt wurde	The motor-car was wrecked without his being hurt
Der Zug kam ſpät an, ſo daß ich eilen mußte	The train arrived late, so that I had to hurry
Der Zug kam ſo ſpät an, daß ich eilen mußte	The train arrived so late that I had to hurry

328. Indem, während, and wogegen.

(a) Indem is generally used when the subjects of the two sentences refer to the same person or thing. The present participle can often be used in the English translation:

Indem er sprach, bemerkte er, daß . . .	While (he was) speaking, he noticed that . . .
Während er sprach, bemerkte ich, daß . . .	While he was speaking, I noticed that . . .

(b) Indem is often used to denote means:

Indem er den ganzen Tag arbeitete, brachte er es am Abend fertig	By working all day, he finished it in the evening

(c) Während, like *while*, is sometimes used to denote a contrast, but for this purpose it is better to use wogegen, *whereas*:

Wilhelm II. war Kaiser, wogegen Hindenburg Präsident war	William II was emperor, whereas Hindenburg was president

329. Indessen and unterdessen are occasionally used instead of indem as conjunctions, but they are more often used as adverbs:

Indessen bemerkte ich, daß . . .	Meanwhile I noticed that . . .

330. Translation of ' after ' and ' afterwards.' Nach (preposition) and nachdem (conjunction) mean *after*, and nachher (adverb) means *after* or *afterwards*:

Zwei Tage nach Weihnachten	Two days after Christmas
Nachdem er gekommen war	After he had come
Nachher war nichts zu sehen	There was nothing to be seen afterwards

331. Ob.

(a) In English, *if* is often loosely used to mean *whether*: *Ask him if (whether) he is coming*. This must be translated by ob, not wenn: Fragen Sie ihn, ob er kommt.

(b) For the use of the subjunctive or indicative after ob, see paragraphs **430** and **432** (a).

332. Obgleich, obschon, obwohl, wenngleich, wennschon. Each of these conjunctions may be used as one word or two:

Obgleich er gekommen ist (or ob er gleich gekommen ist)	Although he has come

333. Translation of 'since.' Seit (preposition and conjunction), seitdem (conjunction and adverb), and seither (adverb) all mean *since*, referring to time, not reason:

Seit seiner Ankunft	Since his arrival
Seit(dem) er angekommen ist	Since he arrived
Seitdem (or seither) ist das nicht geschehen	That has not happened since

334. Tense used with seit and seitdem. For the use of the present or imperfect with seit and seitdem, instead of the English perfect or pluperfect, see paragraph **441** (c).

335. So, used with adverbs.

(a) So is used with adverbs to form the following subordinating conjunctions:[1]

sobald sowie } as soon as	sofern soviel } as far as	
solang(e), as long as	soweit	
sooft, as often as, whenever	so wahr, as sure as	

Sobald er uns sah	As soon as he saw us
Soweit ich es beurteilen kann	As far as I can judge

(b) Sowie, meaning *as well as*, is sometimes used to connect words or phrases (not sentences):

Der Stadtpark enthält Bäume sowie allerlei Blumen	The municipal park contains trees as well as all kinds of flowers

(c) For the use of so with auch to introduce an adverb clause of concession, see paragraph **210** (c).

---

[1] If these expressions are used adverbially, they are better written as two words: Er kam so bald wie möglich, *He came as soon as possible.*

336. Weil and wegen. Weil is a conjunction, meaning *because*; wegen is a preposition, meaning *because of*:

Weil das Wetter schlecht ist	Because the weather is bad
Wegen des schlechten Wetters	Because of the bad weather

337. Wenn.

(a) For the difference between als, wann, and wenn, see paragraph **193**.

(b) Wenn is very often omitted, and the inverted order is then used, as it sometimes is in English. In this construction, the main clause must follow, and must begin with so (or, less often, with dann):

Hätte ich das gewußt, so wäre ich nicht gekommen, or Wenn ich das gewußt hätte, (so) wäre ich usw.	If I had known that (or Had I known that), I should not have come
Ich wäre nicht gekommen, wenn ich das gewußt hätte	I should not have come if I had known that

(c) For the use of the indicative or subjunctive after wenn, see paragraph **435** (a).

338. Wenn auch.

(a) The auch follows a pronoun subject, but generally precedes a noun subject:

Wenn er auch müde ist	Although he is tired
Wenn auch der Junge müde ist	Although the boy is tired

(b) The inverted order may be used instead of wenn, as in paragraph **337** (b). Auch then follows the subject:

Ist der Junge auch müde	Although the boy is tired

339. Wenn nicht. The position of nicht with a noun subject depends on the emphasis[1] [compare paragraph **239**]. It follows a pronoun subject:

Wenn nicht mein Bruder im Zimmer ist	Unless my brother is in the room (emphasis on *brother*)
Wenn mein Bruder nicht im Zimmer ist	Unless my brother is in the room (emphasis on *room*)
Wenn er nicht im Zimmer ist	Unless he is in the room

[1] The same applies to damit nicht, *lest*.

340. Wie.

(a) For the difference between als and wie, meaning *as* or *like*, see paragraph **320** (d).

(b) Wie, although it is a conjunction, may often be translated by the preposition *like*. Two words joined by wie as in the following example usually take the same case, being in apposition (in such sentences the second of the two words is occasionally found in the nominative, being regarded as the subject of some form of sein understood, but this is not usual):

In einer Stadt wie dieser   In a town like this

(c) Wie is sometimes used instead of als to mean *as* (referring to time):

Als (or wie) es nun gegen Abend kam, da bemerkte sie . . .   Now when (or as) it was getting on towards evening, she noticed . . .

(d) For the use of als and wie in comparisons of adjectives and adverbs, see paragraphs **165** and **207**.

(e) For wie as an adverb meaning *how*, see paragraph **241** (e).

341. Adverbs used as conjunctions. The interrogative adverbs wie, *how*; wann, *when*; wo, *where*; and warum, *why*, are used as subordinating conjunctions, often in indirect questions:

Ich weiß nicht, wie (wann, wo, warum) das geschehen ist   I do not know how (when, where, why) that has happened

342. Omission of main clause. In conversation, the main clause is often omitted before a subordinating conjunction:

Ob er noch hier ist?   (I wonder) whether he is still here

Daß er noch hier ist!   Why, he's still here !

343. Additional pronoun or adverb in main clause. It is common in German to put into the main clause an additional pronoun or adverb to anticipate a subordinate clause:

Das kann er nicht verstehen, daß Sie nicht geschrieben haben	He cannot understand your not having written
Er verläßt sich darauf, daß Sie morgen kommen	He is relying on your coming tomorrow
Ich fand ihn da, wo Sie ihn gesehen hatten	I found him where you had seen him

CORRELATIVE CONJUNCTIONS

344. Correlative conjunctions. The following conjunctions are used in pairs, the second of each pair completing the first:

entweder . . . oder . . .	either . . . or . . .
je . . . desto . . . (or je . . . um so . . .)	the . . . the . . .
so . . . so . . .	as . . . as . . .
sowohl . . . als . . .	both . . . and . . .
weder . . . noch . . .	neither . . . nor . . .

(a) Entweder . . . oder . . . If two separate clauses are joined, entweder usually takes the normal order (though the inverted order is sometimes used), and oder the normal order. If there is only one clause, the normal order is used:

Entweder die Uhr geht vor, oder es wird spät	Either the clock is fast or it is getting late
Es gibt entweder Tee oder Kaffee zum Frühstück	There is either tea or coffee for breakfast

(b) Je . . . desto . . . (or je . . . um so . . .). Je introduces an adverb clause, and the verb comes last; desto takes the inverted order:

Je früher die Sonne aufgeht, desto (or um so) später geht sie unter	The earlier the sun rises, the later it sets

(c) So . . . ſo . . . . The first ſo introduces an adverb clause, and the verb comes last: the second ſo takes the inverted order:

So lang das Buch iſt, ſo lang=   The book is as dull as it is
  weilig iſt es (auch)   long

(d) Sowohl . . . als . . . connects either two subjects or objects with one verb, or two verbs with one subject or object. The normal order is used:

Sowohl Berlin als (auch)   Both Berlin and London are
  London ſind Hauptſtädte   capitals

(e) Weder . . . noch . . . The construction is generally as in the preceding section:

Er hat weder geſchrieben noch   He has neither written nor
  geſprochen   spoken

Noch is occasionally used to mean *or* or *nor* after other negatives than weder, but it is generally better to use oder or und nicht:

Ich habe ihn nicht geſehen und   I have not seen him, nor do
  weiß nicht, wo er iſt   I know (or and I do not
    know) where he is

X

VERBS

CONJUGATIONS

345. Haben, *to have.*

Infinitive, haben, to have
Present Participle, habend, having
Past Participle, gehabt, had

Indicative	*Subjunctive*		*Indicative*	*Subjunctive*
Present : I have			*Imperfect :* I had	
ich habe	ich habe		ich hatte	ich hätte
du hast	du habest		du hattest	du hättest
er hat	er habe		er hatte	er hätte
wir haben	wir haben		wir hatten	wir hätten
ihr habt	ihr habet		ihr hattet	ihr hättet
sie haben	sie haben		sie hatten	sie hätten

Perfect : I have had			*Pluperfect :* I had had		
ich habe	ich habe		ich hatte	ich hätte	
du hast	du habest		du hattest	du hättest	
er hat	er habe	gehabt	er hatte	er hätte	gehabt
wir haben	wir haben		wir hatten	wir hätten	
ihr habt	ihr habet		ihr hattet	ihr hättet	
sie haben	sie haben		sie hatten	sie hätten	

Future : I shall have			*Future Perfect :* I shall have had		
ich werde	ich werde		ich werde		ich werde	
du wirst	du werdest		du wirst		du werdest	
er wird	er werde	haben	er wird	gehabt haben	er werde	gehabt haben
wir werden	wir werden		wir werden		wir werden	
ihr werdet	ihr werdet		ihr werdet		ihr werdet	
sie werden	sie werden		sie werden		sie werden	

Indicative

Conditional : I should have	*Conditional Perfect :* I should have had		*Imperative :*	
ich würde	ich würde		habe,	haben wir,
du würdest	du würdest		have	let us have
er würde	er würde	gehabt haben	habt,	er habe,
wir würden	wir würden		have	let him have
ihr würdet	ihr würdet		haben Sie,	haben sie,
sie würden	sie würden		have	let them have

346. Sein, *to be.*

Infinitive, ſein, to be
Present Participle, ſeienb, being
Past Participle, geweſen, been

Indicative	Subjunctive	Indicative	Subjunctive
Present : I am		*Imperfect :* I was	
ich bin	ich ſei	ich war	ich wäre
bu biſt	bu ſei(e)ſt	bu warſt	bu wäreſt
er iſt	er ſei	er war	er wäre
wir ſinb	wir ſeien	wir waren	wir wären
ihr ſeib	ihr ſeiet	ihr wart	ihr wäret
ſie ſinb	ſie ſeien	ſie waren	ſie wären

Indicative	Subjunctive	Indicative	Subjunctive
Perfect : I have been		*Pluperfect :* I had been	
ich bin	ich ſei	ich war	ich wäre
bu biſt	bu ſei(e)ſt	bu warſt	bu wäreſt
er iſt `geweſen`	er ſei `geweſen`	er war `geweſen`	er wäre `geweſen`
wir ſinb	wir ſeien	wir waren	wir wären
ihr ſeib	ihr ſeiet	ihr wart	ihr wäret
ſie ſinb	ſie ſeien	ſie waren	ſie wären

Indicative	Subjunctive	Indicative	Subjunctive
Future : I shall be		*Future Perfect :* I shall have been	
ich werbe	ich werbe	ich werbe	ich werbe
bu wirſt	bu werbeſt	bu wirſt	bu werbeſt
er wirb `ſein`	er werbe `ſein`	er wirb `geweſen ſein`	er werbe `geweſen ſein`
wir werben	wir werben	wir werben	wir werben
ihr werbet	ihr werbet	ihr werbet	ihr werbet
ſie werben	ſie werben	ſie werben	ſie werben

Indicative

Conditional : I should be	Conditional Perfect : I should have been	Imperative :	
ich würbe	ich würbe	ſei,	ſeien wir,
bu würbeſt	bu würbeſt	be	let us be
er würbe `ſein`	er würbe `geweſen ſein`	ſeib,	er ſei,
wir würben	wir würben	be	let him be
ihr würbet	ihr würbet	ſeien Sie,	ſeien ſie,
ſie würben	ſie würben	be	let them be

347. Werden, *to become.*

Infinitive, werben, to become
Present Participle, werbenb, becoming
Past Participle, geworben, become

Indicative	*Subjunctive*	*Indicative*	*Subjunctive*
Present : I become		Imperfect : I became	
ich werbe	ich werbe	ich wurbe	ich würbe
bu wirft	bu werbeft	bu wurbeft	bu würbeft
er wirb	er werbe	er wurbe	er würbe
wir werben	wir werben	wir wurben	wir würben
ihr werbet	ihr werbet	ihr wurbet	ihr würbet
sie werben	sie werben	sie wurben	sie würben

Perfect : I have become				*Pluperfect :* I had become			
ich bin		ich sei		ich war		ich wäre	
bu bift		bu sei(e)ft		bu warst		bu wärest	
er ist	geworben	er sei	geworben	er war	geworben	er wäre	geworben
wir sinb		wir seien		wir waren		wir wären	
ihr seib		ihr seiet		ihr wart		ihr wäret	
sie sinb		sie seien		sie waren		sie wären	

Future : I shall become				*Future Perfect :* I shall have become			
ich werbe		ich werbe		ich werbe		ich werbe	
bu wirft		bu werbeft		bu wirft		bu werbeft	
er wirb	werben	er werbe	werben	er wirb	geworben sein	er werbe	geworben sein
wir werben		wir werben		wir werben		wir werben	
ihr werbet		ihr werbet		ihr werbet		ihr werbet	
sie werben		sie werben		sie werben		sie werben	

Indicative

Conditional : I should become		*Conditional Perfect :* I should have become		*Imperative :*	
ich würbe		ich würbe		werbe,	werben wir,
bu würbeft		bu würbeft		become	let us become
er würbe	werben	er würbe	geworben sein	werbet,	er werbe,
wir würben		wir würben		become	let him become
ihr würbet		ihr würbet		werben Sie,	werben sie,
sie würben		sie würben		become	let them become

348. Bauen, *to build.* (Weak verb.)

Infinitive, bauen, to build
Present Participle, bauend, building
Past Participle, gebaut, built

Indicative	*Subjunctive*	*Indicative and Subjunctive*
Present : I build		*Imperfect :* I built
ich baue	ich baue	ich baute
du baust	du bauest	du bautest
er baut	er baue	er baute
wir bauen	wir bauen	wir bauten
ihr baut	ihr bauet	ihr bautet
sie bauen	sie bauen	sie bauten

Perfect : I have built

				Pluperfect : I had built			
ich habe	ich habe			ich hatte	ich hätte		
du hast	du habest			du hattest	du hättest		
er hat	er habe	gebaut		er hatte	er hätte	gebaut	
wir haben	wir haben			wir hatten	wir hätten		
ihr habt	ihr habet			ihr hattet	ihr hättet		
sie haben	sie haben			sie hatten	sie hätten		

Future : I shall build

				Future Perfect : I shall have built			
ich werde	ich werde			ich werde		ich werde	
du wirst	du werdest			du wirst		du werdest	
er wird	er werde	bauen		er wird	gebaut haben	er werde	gebaut haben
wir werden	wir werden			wir werden		wir werden	
ihr werdet	ihr werdet			ihr werdet		ihr werdet	
sie werden	sie werden			sie werden		sie werden	

Indicative

Conditional : I should build	*Conditional Perfect :* I should have built		*Imperative :*	
ich würde	ich würde		baue,	bauen wir,
du würdest	du würdest		build	let us build
er würde	er würde	gebaut haben	baut,	er baue,
wir würden	wir würden		build	let him build
ihr würdet	ihr würdet		bauen Sie,	bauen sie,
sie würden	sie würden		build	let them build

349. Geben, *to give.* (Strong verb.)

Infinitive, geben, to give
Present Participle, gebend, giving
Past Participle, gegeben, given

Indicative	*Subjunctive*	*Indicative*	*Subjunctive*
Present : I give		*Imperfect :* I gave	
ich gebe	ich gebe	ich gab	ich gäbe
du gibst	du gebest	du gabst	du gäbest
er gibt	er gebe	er gab	er gäbe
wir geben	wir geben	wir gaben	wir gäben
ihr gebt	ihr gebet	ihr gabt	ihr gäbet
sie geben	sie geben	sie gaben	sie gäben

	Perfect : I have given			*Pluperfect :* I had given	
ich habe	ich habe		ich hatte	ich hätte	
du hast	du habest		du hattest	du hättest	
er hat	er habe	gegeben	er hatte	er hätte	gegeben
wir haben	wir haben		wir hatten	wir hätten	
ihr habt	ihr habet		ihr hattet	ihr hättet	
sie haben	sie haben		sie hatten	sie hätten	

	Future : I shall give			*Future Perfect :* I shall have given	
ich werde	ich werde		ich werde	ich werde	
du wirst	du werdest		du wirst	du werdest	
er wird	er werde	geben	er wird	er werde	gegeben haben
wir werden	wir werden		wir werden	wir werden	
ihr werdet	ihr werdet		ihr werdet	ihr werdet	
sie werden	sie werden		sie werden	sie werden	

Indicative

Conditional : I should give	*Conditional Perfect :* I should have given	*Imperative :*	
ich würde	ich würde	gib,	geben wir,
du würdest	du würdest	give	let us give
er würde	er würde	gebt,	er gebe,
wir würden	wir würden	give	let him give
ihr würdet	ihr würdet	geben Sie,	geben sie,
sie würden	sie würden	give	let them give

350. Fallen, *to fall.* (Conjugated with ſein.)

Infinitive, faÏÏen, to fall
Present Participle, faÏÏenb, falling
Past Participle, gefaÏÏen, fallen

Indicative	Subjunctive	Indicative	Subjunctive
Present : I fall		Imperfect : I fell	
ich faÏÏe	ich faÏÏe	ich fiel	ich fiele
bu fäÏÏſt	bu faÏÏeſt	bu fielſt	bu fieleſt
er fäÏÏt	er faÏÏe	er fiel	er fiele
wir faÏÏen	wir faÏÏen	wir fielen	wir fielen
ihr faÏÏt	ihr faÏÏet	ihr fielt	ihr fielet
ſie faÏÏen	ſie faÏÏen	ſie fielen	ſie fielen

Perfect : I have fallen		Pluperfect : I had fallen	
ich bin	ich ſei	ich war	ich wäre
bu biſt	bu ſei(e)ſt	bu warſt	bu wäreſt
er iſt	er ſei	er war	er wäre
wir ſinb	wir ſeien	wir waren	wir wären
ihr ſeib	ihr ſeiet	ihr wart	ihr wäret
ſie ſinb	ſie ſeien	ſie waren	ſie wären

(gefaÏÏen)

Future : I shall fall		Future Perfect : I shall have fallen	
ich werbe	ich werbe	ich werbe	ich werbe
bu wirſt	bu werbeſt	bu wirſt	bu werbeſt
er wirb	er werbe	er wirb	er werbe
wir werben	wir werben	wir werben	wir werben
ihr werbet	ihr werbet	ihr werbet	ihr werbet
ſie werben	ſie werben	ſie werben	ſie werben

(faÏÏen / gefaÏÏen ſein)

Indicative

Conditional : I should fall	Conditional Perfect : I should have fallen	Imperative :	
ich würbe	ich würbe	faÏÏe,	faÏÏen wir,
bu würbeſt	bu würbeſt	fall	let us fall
er würbe	er würbe	faÏÏt,	er faÏÏe,
wir würben	wir würben	fall	let him fall
ihr würbet	ihr würbet	faÏÏen Sie,	faÏÏen ſie,
ſie würben	ſie würben	fall	let them fall

(faÏÏen / gefaÏÏen ſein)

351. Loben, *to praise.* (Conjugated in the passive.)

Infinitive, gelobt werden, to be praised

There are no passive participles formed with werden; for a special present participle, used adjectivally, see paragraph **423**.

Indicative	*Subjunctive*		*Indicative*	*Subjunctive*	
Present : I am praised			*Imperfect :* I was praised		
ich werde	ich werde		ich wurde	ich würde	
du wirst	du werdest		du wurdest	du würdest	
er wird	er werde	gelobt	er wurde	er würde	gelobt
wir werden	wir werden		wir wurden	wir würden	
ihr werdet	ihr werdet		ihr wurdet	ihr würdet	
sie werden	sie werden		sie wurden	sie würden	

Perfect : I have been praised			*Pluperfect :* I had been praised		
ich bin	ich sei		ich war	ich wäre	
du bist	du sei(e)st		du warst	du wärest	
er ist	er sei	gelobt worden	er war	er wäre	gelobt worden
wir sind	wir seien		wir waren	wir wären	
ihr seid	ihr seiet		ihr wart	ihr wäret	
sie sind	sie seien		sie waren	sie wären	

Future : I shall be praised			*Future Perfect :* I shall have been praised		
ich werde	ich werde		ich werde	ich werde	
du wirst	du werdest		du wirst	du werdest	
er wird	er werde	gelobt werden	er wird	er werde	gelobt worden sein
wir werden	wir werden		wir werden	wir werden	
ihr werdet	ihr werdet		ihr werdet	ihr werdet	
sie werden	sie werden		sie werden	sie werden	

Indicative

Conditional : I should be praised			*Conditional Perfect :* I should have been praised			*Imperative :*	
ich würde			ich würde			werde, werdet, werden Sie gelobt, be praised	
du würdest			du würdest				
er würde		gelobt worden	er würde		gelobt worden sein	werden wir gelobt	let us, let
wir würden			wir würden			er werde gelobt	him, let
ihr würdet			ihr würdet			werden sie gelobt	them be
sie würden			sie würden				praised

352. Modal auxiliary verbs.

dürfen, to be allowed   müssen, to be obliged
können, to be able   sollen, to owe
mögen, to like   wollen, to wish

Past Participle[1]

| gedurft | gekonnt | gemocht | gemußt | gesollt | gewollt |

Present Indicative

ich	darf	kann	mag	muß	soll	will
du	darfst	kannst	magst	mußt	sollst	willst
er	darf	kann	mag	muß	soll	will
wir	dürfen	können	mögen	müssen	sollen	wollen
ihr	dürft	könnt	mögt	müßt	sollt	wollt
sie	dürfen	können	mögen	müssen	sollen	wollen

Present Subjunctive

| ich | dürfe | könne | möge | müsse | solle | wolle |

Imperfect Indicative

| ich | durfte | konnte | mochte | mußte | sollte | wollte |

Imperfect Subjunctive

| ich | dürfte | könnte | möchte | müßte | sollte | wollte |

Conditional[2]

ich	dürfte	könnte	möchte	müßte	sollte	wollte or
						würde
						wollen

Conditional Perfect or Pluperfect Subjunctive

ich hätte gedurft, gekonnt, gemocht, gemußt, gesollt, gewollt

Meanings. The meanings given above often have to be varied. See paragraphs **389** ff.

---

[1] For the use of the infinitive instead of the past participle, see paragraph **385**.

[2] Except in the present conditional of wollen, the auxiliary werden is not used to form the conditional of these verbs; see paragraph **428**

FORMATION OF TENSES

353. The infinitive of most verbs ends in ⸗en. A few end in ⸗n (ſein, *to be*; ħandeln, *to act*; dauern, *to last*).

354. The principal parts are generally taken to be the infinitive, the first person singular of the imperfect, and the past participle; thus:

> *Weak:* bauen, baute, gebaut, to build
> *Strong:* geben, gab, gegeben, to give

355. The present participle has the form of the infinitive with ⸗d added: bauend, *building*; gebend, *giving*; lächelnd, *smiling*.

356. For the gerund, the infinitive is used, and not the present participle: Das Radfaħren wird leicht gelernt, *Cycling is easily learnt.*

357. The past participle of weak verbs consists of **ge**+ stem+**t**.[1] The past participle of strong verbs consists of **ge** +stem+**en,** the stem vowel often being changed: bauen, gebaut; geben, gegeben; ſingen, geſungen.

358. The present subjunctive is formed by adding ⸗e to the stem of the infinitive: bauen, ich baue; geben, ich gebe. The present and imperfect subjunctive have the same endings, all of which contain an **e.**

359. The imperfect indicative of weak verbs is formed by adding ⸗te to the stem. In strong verbs it is formed by changing the stem vowel, there being no additional ending in the first and third person singular: ich baute; ich ħandelte; ich gab.

---

[1] See paragraph **373** for verbs that do not add ge⸗ in the past participle.

360. The imperfect subjunctive is the same in weak verbs as the imperfect indicative. In strong verbs, the endings of the present subjunctive are added to the stem of the imperfect indicative, the stem vowel **a, o,** or **u** being modified. In some strong verbs there is a choice between two vowels; see paragraph **379.**

361. The future is formed by the present of werden and the infinitive: ich werde bauen; ich werde geben.

362. The conditional is formed by the imperfect subjunctive of werden and the infinitive: ich würde bauen; ich würde geben. For the use of the imperfect subjunctive for the conditional, especially with the auxiliary verbs of mood, see paragraph **428.**

363. Sein instead of haben. It should be remembered that many verbs take sein, not haben, as the auxiliary in compound tenses [see paragraph **411**]:

Ich habe gebaut	I have built
Ich bin gekommen	I have come
Ich hatte gebaut	I had built
Ich war gekommen	I had come
Ich werde gebaut haben	I shall have built
Ich werde gekommen sein	I shall have come

364. Familiar and formal forms: du, ihr, and Sie. *You build* may be du baust, ihr baut, or Sie bauen (Sie taking the same form of the verb as sie). For the difference between these pronouns, see paragraph **69.**

365. The imperative.

(a) The usual forms are:

baue, build (familiar form, singular)
baut, build (familiar form, plural)
bauen Sie, build (formal form, singular and plural)

(b) The **e** of the familiar form singular (baue) is often dropped, especially in very common words such as gehen, *to go*; kommen, *to come*; and lassen, *to let*.[1] For the strong verbs in which it must be dropped, see paragraph **375.**

---

[1] In lassen the e must be dropped: laß.

(c) Laſſen or wollen may be used for the first person plural of the imperative; thus, *let us build* may be bauen wir, laß (laßt or laſſen Sie) uns bauen, or wir wollen bauen.

(d) Laſſen or ſollen may be used for the third person singular or plural of the imperative: laß, laßt, or laſſen Sie ihn bauen, or er ſoll bauen, *let him build*; laß, laßt, or laſſen Sie ſie bauen, or ſie ſollen bauen, *let them build*.

For the use of man with the third person singular of the imperative, see paragraph **123** (c).

(e) An exclamation mark is generally used with the imperative: Kommen Sie bald wieder! *Come again soon.*

366. Substitutes for the imperative.

(a) The infinitive is often used, especially in requests of a general and formal nature:

(Bitte) wenden!	Please turn over
Nicht hinauslehnen!	Do not put your head out of the window

(b) The past participle is also used, generally in more abrupt orders:

Aufgepaßt!	Look out!
Stillgeſtanden!	Stand still!

367. Omission of the auxiliaries haben and ſein.

(a) When a finite form of haben or ſein comes at the end of a sentence after a past participle, it is sometimes omitted:

Und eh' die drei Jäger ihn recht geſeh'n,	And before the three huntsmen had really seen him, etc.
So war er davon über Tiefen und Höh'n	

(b) This omission is not usually made in the conversational style. It should be avoided if the past participle has the same form as any other part of the verb (*e.g.*, verbeſſert is both past participle and third person singular present indicative).

368. Continuous forms. There are no continuous forms in the German tenses. Care should be taken not to use the verb ſein or the present participle in such constructions as:

Present: ich baue, I build, or I am building

Imperfect: ich baute, I built, or I was building

Future: ich werde bauen, I shall build, or I shall be building

Perfect: ich habe gebaut, I have built, or I have been building

369. Negative and interrogative forms.

(a) The negative is expressed by nicht, which is put after the auxiliary or finite verb, but before the infinitive or past participle. The verb *to do*, used as an auxiliary, is not translated:[1]

Ich baue nicht	I do not build
Ich baute nicht	I did not build
Ich habe nicht gebaut	I have not built

(b) The interrogative is expressed by inversion, whether the subject is a noun or a pronoun:

Baue ich (nicht)?	Do I (not) build?
Baut mein Vater (nicht)?	Does (not) my father build?
Baute ich (nicht)?	Did I (not) build?
Habe ich (nicht) gebaut?	Have I (not) built?

SPECIAL FORMS OF CERTAIN WEAK VERBS

370. Verbs with stems ending in =d or =t (*e.g.*, reden, *to talk*; arbeiten, *to work*), or by =m or =n preceded by another consonant (*e.g.*, atmen, *to breathe*; rechnen, *to reckon*), keep an e before all endings:

Present Indicative		*Imperfect*	*Past Participle*
ich rede	wir reden	ich redete	geredet
du redeſt	ihr redet		
er redet	ſie reden		

371. Verbs ending in =eln (*e.g.*, handeln, *to act*) have slight irregularities in the present indicative, present

---

[1] The verbs *to have, to be,* and *to do* are not used alone as auxiliaries in German, as they are in English: Ich ſuche A. —Ich auch, *I am looking for A.—So am I.*

subjunctive, and imperative, which are usually as follows:[1]

Present Indicative		*Present Subjunctive*	
ich handle	wir handeln	ich handle	wir handeln
du handelst	ihr handelt	du handelst	ihr handelt
er handelt	sie handeln	er handle	sie handeln

Imperative: handle, handelt, handeln Sie

372. Verbs with stems ending in a sibilant (*e.g.*, reisen, *to travel*; wischen, *to wipe*; boxen, *to box*; heizen, *to heat*) may add an **e** in the second person singular; but this form is often shortened to that of the third person singular, except with stems ending in **=sch,** which should keep the extra ſ:

Present Indicative			
ich reise	wir reisen	ich wische	wir wischen
du reis(es)t	ihr reist	du wisch(e)st	ihr wischt
er reist	sie reisen	er wischt	sie wischen

373. Past participle. Verbs ending in **=ieren** (all weak) (*e.g.*, studieren, *to study*) and verbs (weak or strong) with inseparable prefixes (*e.g.*, bemerken, *to notice*; gefallen, *to please*) do not add an extra **ge=** in the past participle:

Infinitive	*Past Participle*
studieren, to study	studiert
bekommen, to get	bekommen
bemerken, to notice	bemerkt
gefallen, to please	gefallen

SPECIAL FORMS OF CERTAIN STRONG VERBS

374. Strong verbs with the stem vowel a or au (*e.g.*, fallen, *to fall*; laufen, *to run*).

(a) Most of these modify in the second and third person singular of the present indicative:

ich falle	wir fallen	ich laufe	wir laufen
du fällst	ihr fallt	du läufst	ihr lauft
er fällt	sie fallen	er läuft	sie laufen

[1] These slight contractions are also sometimes made with verbs ending in =ern: ich klett(e)re, *I climb*.

(b) The exceptions, which do not modify, are:

ſchaffen, to create	hauen, to hew
ſchallen, to resound	ſaugen, to suck

375. Strong verbs with the stem vowel e (*e.g.*, brechen, *to break*; befehlen, *to command*).

(a) In most of these verbs the stem vowel **e** changes into **i** or **ie** in the second and third person singular of the present indicative. Those that change into **i** are (1) those with a short vowel (*e.g.*, brechen, *to break*), (2) those with **er** before a consonant in the stem (*e.g.*, werfen, *to throw*), and (3) geben, *to give*; nehmen (nimmſt, nimmt), *to take*; and treten (trittſt, tritt), *to step*:

ich breche	wir brechen	ich befehle	wir befehlen
du brichſt	ihr brecht	du befiehlſt	ihr befehlt
er bricht	ſie brechen	er befiehlt	ſie befehlen

(b) These verbs change the stem vowel in the same way in the second person singular of the imperative, and drop the final =e:

brich, brecht, brechen Sie   befiehl, befehlt, befehlen Sie

(c) The exceptions, which do not change the vowel, are:

gehen, to go	heben, to lift	bewegen, to induce
ſtehen, to stand	weben, to weave	geneſen, to recover

376. Strong verbs with the stem vowel o. There are only two of these: ſtoßen, *to push*, which modifies like fallen [paragraph **374 (a)**]; and kommen, *to come*, which does not modify.

377. Strong verbs with stems ending in =d or =t.

(a) Those that do not modify or change the vowel in the present indicative (*e.g.*, leiden, *to suffer*) are conjugated like reden (paragraph **370**).

(b) Those that modify or change the vowel in the present indicative (*e.g.*, halten, *to hold*; fechten, *to fight*) do not add =e in the second person singular, or =et in the third:

ich halte	wir halten	ich fechte	wir fechten
du hältſt	ihr haltet	du fichtſt	ihr fechtet
er hält	ſie halten	er ficht	ſie fechten

378. Strong verbs with stems ending in a sibilant are conjugated as in paragraph **372**, subject to any modification or change of vowel.

379. The imperfect subjunctive of some strong and irregular verbs is slightly irregular:

Infinitive	Imp. Subj.	Infinitive	Imp. Subj.
(a)			
brennen	brennte	rennen	rennte
kennen	kennte	senden	sendete
nennen	nennte	wenden	wendete
(b)			
befehlen	beföhle	beginnen	begönne[1]
empfehlen	empföhle	schwimmen	schwömme[1]
bersten	börste[1]	sinnen	sönne[1]
gelten	gölte[1]	spinnen	spönne[1]
schelten	schölte[1]		
(c)			
helfen	hülfe[1]	sterben	stürbe
schwören	schwüre[2]	verderben	verdürbe
stehen	stände[3]	werben	würbe
		werfen	würfe

(d) Of the modal auxiliary verbs, those that modify the vowel in the infinitive also modify it in the imperfect subjunctive. Sollen and wollen do not modify.

MODAL AUXILIARY VERBS, AND Lassen

380. The modal auxiliary verbs are dürfen, können, mögen, müssen, sollen, and wollen; they are conjugated in paragraph **352**. Lassen is conjugated in paragraph **408**.

---

[1] Alternative form with ä (bärste, etc.).
[2] Alternative form schwöre.   [3] Alternative form stünde.

381. Like the auxiliary verbs haben, sein, and werden, they may be used as independent verbs, or with other verbs:

Wollen Sie Tinte?	Do you want some ink?
Wollen Sie Tinte kaufen?	Do you want to buy some ink?

382. They take the same place as haben, sein, and werden in relation to the verb with which they are used:

Wenn er Tinte gekauft hat	If he has bought some ink
Wenn er Tinte kaufen will	If he wants to buy some ink

383. The infinitive without zu.

(a) An infinitive depending on these verbs does not take zu:

Ich will Tinte kaufen	I want to buy some ink
Lassen Sie das bleiben	Leave that alone
Ich mußte hinausgehen	I had to go out

(b) For other verbs followed by an infinitive without zu, see paragraph **417**.

384. Use of zu with the modal auxiliaries. These verbs, although followed by an infinitive without zu, take zu with their own infinitives when the construction needs it:

Es ist nützlich, schwimmen zu können	It is useful to be able to swim
Ich erwarte, einen Brief schreiben zu müssen	I expect to have to write a letter

385. Infinitive for past participle.

(a) The past participle of the modal auxiliaries and lassen, when used with the infinitive of another verb, takes the form of an infinitive (really a strong form of the past participle):

Ich habe es tun können	I have been able to do it
Ich habe es tun müssen	I have had to do it
Ich habe es tun wollen	I have wanted to do it

(b) This construction is generally used with the verbs fühlen, *to feel*; heißen, *to bid*; hören, *to hear*; lehren, *to teach*, lernen, *to learn*; and sehen, *to see*:

Wir haben ihn kommen hören,   We heard, saw him come
   sehen

(c) If the verb has no dependent infinitive, the ordinary form of the past participle is used:

Ich habe es nicht gekonnt   I have not been able (to do it)

Ich habe es nicht gesehen   I have not seen it

(d) The auxiliary verbs of mood may be used in the present tense with the past participle of another verb, as in English. The following examples show this construction and that given in section **(a)**:

Er muß es getan haben   He must have done it
Er hat es tun müssen   He has had to do it
Er kann es getan haben   He may have done it
Er hat es tun können   He has been able to do it

386. The conditional perfect, or pluperfect subjunctive.

(a) With dürfen, mögen, müssen, and wollen the translation is straightforward:

Ich hätte es tun dürfen   I should have been allowed to do it

Ich hätte es tun mögen   I should have liked to do it

Ich hätte es tun müssen   I should have had (or been obliged) to do it

Ich hätte es tun wollen   I should have wanted to do it

(b) With können and sollen a slightly different English construction is needed, the dependent present infinitive being translated by the perfect infinitive:

Ich hätte es tun können   I could have done it (or I should have been able to do it)

Ich hätte es tun sollen   I ought to have done it

387. Order of words. When two infinitive forms come together in a subordinate sentence, the finite verb comes immediately before the first infinitive:

Weil ich den Brief habe schreiben müssen	Because I have had to write the letter
Ich weiß nicht, ob ich den Brief werde schreiben müssen	I do not know whether I shall have to write the letter
Obgleich er gestern hätte kommen sollen	Although he ought to have come yesterday

388. Examples of the modal verbs. The following paragraphs give the principal meanings of the modal verbs and lassen.

389. Dürfen denotes permission (1-3), or, in the negative, a prohibition (4), or, in the imperfect subjunctive, possibility (5):

Darf ich fragen, ob . . .?	May I ask whether . . .?
Das darf er (tun)	He may (or is allowed to) do that
Das durfte er (tun)	He was allowed to do that
Das dürfen Sie nicht (tun)	You must not do that
Das dürfte wahr sein[1]	That might be true

390. Können.

(a) **Können** denotes possibility (1 and 2), ability (3 and 4), or knowledge[2] (5):

Das kann wahr sein	That may be true
Das könnte wahr sein	That might be true
Ich kann es nicht verstehen	I cannot understand it
Er kann sehr schnell laufen	He can run very fast
Können Sie Deutsch?[3]	Do you know German?

---

[1] Das könnte wahr sein would be better.
[2] For *to know*, see kennen and wissen, paragraph **406**, note.
[3] In this usage, referring to languages, sprechen is understood.

(b) When translating *could*, the conditional or the imperfect indicative must be used according to the meaning:

Er könnte es nicht tun, wenn er wollte	He could not (*i.e.*, would not be able to) do it if he wanted to
Er konnte es nicht tun, als er wollte	He could not (*i.e.*, was not able to) do it when he wanted to

391. Mögen denotes possibility (1 and 2), inclination or liking (3, 4, and 5), concession (6), or wish (7 and 8):

Das mag (or kann) wahr sein	That may be true
Er mochte zehn Jahre alt sein	He might (at that time) be ten years old
Ich mag das Haus nicht	I do not like the house
Ich mochte das Haus nicht	I did not like the house
Ich möchte (gern) wissen, ob . . .	I should like to know whether . . .
Mag er auch reich sein	Even though he may be rich
Möge das wahr sein!	May that be true!
Möchte das wahr sein!	Would that that were true!

392. Müssen.

(a) Müssen denotes some kind of compulsion. In future and past tenses it is generally translated by *to have to*, or *to be obliged to*:

Das muß schwer sein	That must be difficult
Ich muß nach Hause (gehen)	I must go home
Ich werde nach Hause (gehen) müssen	I shall have to go home
Ich mußte nach Hause (gehen)	I had to go home
Ich mußte lachen	I could not help laughing

(b) The difference between müssen and haben zu is as follows:

Ich muß einen Brief schreiben	I have to write a letter
Ich habe einen Brief zu schreiben	I have a letter to write

(c) The negative of müſſen is used in two senses: *must not* and *need not*. In order to be clear, it is generally better to use different verbs:

Das dürfen Sie nicht tun	You must not do that
Das brauchen Sie nicht zu tun	You need not do that

393. Sollen.

(a) Sollen in the present tense denotes intention or obligation (1), command (2 and 3), or a suggestion of other people's opinion (4) [see also paragraph **365 (d)** for its use as imperative]:

Ich ſoll morgen abreiſen	I am to leave tomorrow
Du ſollſt nicht töten	Thou shalt not kill
Er ſoll uns nicht ſtören	He shall not (or is not to) disturb us
Herr A. ſoll reich ſein	Mr. A. is said (or supposed) to be rich

(b) The imperfect indicative (1) and imperfect subjunctive (2 and 3) have the same form, but different meanings:

Ich ſollte geſtern abreiſen	I was to leave yesterday
Ich ſollte morgen abreiſen	I ought to leave tomorrow
Wenn er heute abend kommen ſollte	If he should (or were to) come this evening

(c) *Shall* and *should*. *Shall*, if used simply to denote a future state or action, is translated by the future (1); if it denotes intention or command, it is translated by ſollen (2).

Should, if it is used simply to denote a conditional state or action, is translated by the conditional (3); if it denotes duty or possibility, it is translated by ſollen [4, and 3 of section **(b)**]:

Wir werden ihn nicht ſtören	We shall not disturb him
Er ſoll uns nicht ſtören	He shall not disturb us
Ich würde das nicht tun	I should not do that (unless I had to)
Er ſollte das nicht tun	He should not do that (because it is dangerous)

394. Wollen.

(a) Wollen denotes a wish, willingness, or intention (1-3), assertion or pretence (4), or an impending occurrence

—generally used with eben, *just* (5 and 6; with this meaning it may be used of things without life):

Wollen Sie Brot?	Do you want some bread?
So Gott will	D.V.
Wollen Sie mit (kommen)?	Will you come with (me, etc.)?
Er will nichts gehört haben	He asserts (or pretends) that he has heard nothing
Er wollte eben fort	He was just going
Das Feuer wollte eben aus= gehen	The fire was nearly out

(**b**) *Will* and *Would*. *Will*, if used simply to denote a future state or action, is translated by the future (1); if it denotes will or intention, it is translated by wollen (2).

Would, if used simply to denote a conditional state or action, is translated by the conditional (3); if it denotes will or intention, it is translated by wollen (4); if it denotes habitual action, it is translated by the imperfect, or by the verb pflegen, *to be accustomed to* (5):

Er wird uns nicht stören	He will not disturb us
Ich will ihn nicht stören	I will not disturb him
Er würde das nicht tun	He would not do that (if he were asked to)
Er wollte das nicht tun	He would not do that (when he was asked to)
Abends pflegte er zu lesen (or Abends las er)	He would (or used to) read in the evening

395. Lassen.

(**a**) Lassen means *to let* or *allow* (1 and 2) or *to leave*[1] (3) [see also paragraph **365** (**c**) and (**d**) for its use as imperative]:

Laß uns spazieren gehen	Let us go for a walk
Laß mich dir helfen	Let me (or allow me to) help you
Ich ließ das Buch auf dem Tisch liegen[1]	I left the book (lying) on the table

[1] Lassen in this sense means to leave a thing where it is; *to quit* or *abandon* is verlassen: Er hat die Stadt verlassen, *He has left the town*.

(b) It is used reflexively, in the general sense of *to let*:

Das läßt sich denken	That is quite likely
Es läßt sich sehen, hören	It is worth seeing, hearing
Es läßt sich nicht leugnen	It cannot be denied

(c) An active infinitive after lassen must often be translated by the passive:

Er läßt (sich) ein Haus bauen	He is having a house built (for himself)
Er hat (sich) ein Haus bauen lassen	He has had a house built (for himself)

(d) The following sentences illustrate the accusative and dative after lassen. In the first example mich is the direct object of lassen, and in the second example mir is the indirect object of schreiben:

Er ließ mich einen Brief schreiben	He made me write a letter
Er ließ mir einen Brief schreiben	He had a letter written to me

(e) *To let* and *to make*. Lassen may imply permission or compulsion, and is more often used than machen before other verbs. Er ließ mich warten may mean *He let me wait* or *He made me wait*. The meaning may be made more precise by using erlauben, *to allow*; zwingen, *to compel*; or veranlassen, *to cause*:

Er erlaubte mir zu warten	He allowed me to wait
Er zwang mich zu warten	He compelled me to wait
Das schlechte Wetter veranlaßte ihn zu warten	The bad weather caused him to wait

(f) *To make*, before an adjective, is machen:

Das macht es unmöglich	That makes it impossible

STRONG AND IRREGULAR VERBS

396. Classes of strong and irregular verbs. The following is a list of the most important strong and irregular verbs, arranged by classes.

The parts given in the examples are (1) the infinitive, (2) the third person singular present indicative, (3) the first person singular imperfect, (4) the past participle, and (5) the second person singular imperative.

For the contraction of the second person singular of the present indicative of verbs ending in a sibilant (*e.g.*, lefen, *to read*; beißen, *to bite*), see paragraph **372.**

Further details are given in the alphabetical list [paragraph **408**].

397. Class 1 (a, e). Geben, *to give*; lefen, *to read*; and genefen, *to recover*.

(a)	geben	gibt	gab	gegeben	gib
(b)	lefen	lieft	las	gelefen	lies
(c)	genefen	geneft	genas	genefen	genefe

(a)

effen,[1] to eat	meffen, to measure
freffen, to eat (of animals)	treten,[2] to step
geben, to give	vergeffen, to forget

(b)

gefchehen,[3] to happen	fehen,[4] to see
lefen, to read	

(c)

bitten,[5] to ask, request	liegen, to lie
genefen, to recover	fitzen,[5] to sit

398. Class 2 (a, o). Brechen, *to break*; befehlen, *to command*; and beginnen, *to begin*.

(a)	brechen	bricht	brach	gebrochen	brich
(b)	befehlen	befiehlt	befahl	befohlen	befiehl
(c)	beginnen	beginnt	begann	begonnen	beginne

---

[1] Past participle: gegeffen. [2] Present indicative: tritt.
[3] Impersonal. [4] Imperative: fieh or fiehe.
[5] Imperfect and past participle: bat, gebeten; faß, gefeffen.

(a)

bergen, to save
bersten,[1] to burst
brechen, to break
erschrecken,[2] to be frightened
gelten,[1] to be worth
helfen, to help
nehmen,[3] to take
schelten,[1] to scold

sprechen, to speak
stechen, to sting
sterben, to die
treffen,[4] to meet, hit
verbergen, to hide
verderben, to spoil
werben, to woo
werfen, to throw

(b)

befehlen, to command
empfehlen, to recommend

gebären, to bear (children)
stehlen, to steal

(c)

beginnen, to begin
gewinnen, to win
kommen,[4] to come
rinnen, to flow

schwimmen, to swim
sinnen, to meditate
spinnen, to spin

399. Class 3 (a, u). Singen, *to sing.*

Singen singt sang gesungen singe

binden, to bind
dringen, to penetrate
finden, to find
gelingen,[5] to succeed
klingen, to sound
ringen, to wrestle
schlingen, to sling
schwingen, to swing

singen, to sing
sinken, to sink
springen, to jump
trinken, to drink
verschwinden, to disappear
winden, to wind
zwingen, to force

400. Class 4 (i, i). Beißen, *to bite;* greifen, *to grasp;* and gleiten, *to glide.* Verbs with a stem ending in =f or =t double this consonant in the imperfect and past participle.

beißen	beißt	biß	gebissen	beiße
greifen	greift	griff	gegriffen	greife
gleiten	gleitet	glitt	geglitten	gleite

[1] Present indicative: birst, gilt, schilt. [2] Imperfect: erschrak.
[3] Present indicative: nimmt; past participle: genommen.
[4] Imperfect: traf, kam. [5] Impersonal.

beißen, to bite
erbleichen, to fade away
gleichen, to resemble
gleiten, to glide
greifen, to grasp
kneifen, to pinch
leiden,[1] to suffer
pfeifen, to whistle
reißen, to tear

reiten, to ride
schleichen, to sneak
schleifen, to grind
schmeißen, to fling
schneiden,[1] to cut
schreiten, to stride
streichen, to stroke
streiten, to quarrel
weichen, to give way

401. Class 5 (ie, ie). Bleiben, *to remain.*

Bleiben   bleibt   blieb   geblieben   bleibe

bleiben, to remain
gedeihen, to thrive
leihen, to lend
meiden, to shun
preisen, to praise
reiben, to rub
scheiden, to part
scheinen, to shine, seem

schreiben, to write
schreien, to scream
schweigen, to be silent
speien, to spit
steigen, to mount
treiben, to drive
verzeihen, to pardon
weisen, to show

402. Class 6 (ie, root vowel). Blasen, *to blow;* and stoßen, *to push.*

blasen   bläst   blies   geblasen   blase
stoßen   stößt   stieß   gestoßen   stoße

blasen, to blow
braten,[2] to roast
fallen,[3] to fall
fangen,[4] to catch
halten,[2] to hold
hangen,[4] to hang
hauen,[5] to hew

heißen, to be called
lassen, to let
laufen, to run
raten,[2] to advise
rufen,[6] to call
schlafen, to sleep
stoßen, to push

---

[1] Change d into tt in the imperfect and past participle: litt, gelitten; and schnitt, geschnitten.
[2] Present indicative: brät, hält, rät.   [3] Imperfect: fiel.
[4] Imperfect: fing, hing.
[5] Present indicative: haut; imperfect: hieb.
[6] Present indicative: ruft.

403. Class 7 (o, o). Biegen, *to bend*; and ſchwellen, *to swell*.

(a) biegen   biegt   bog   gebogen   biege
(b) ſchwellen   ſchwillt   ſchwoll   geſchwollen   ſchwill

(a)

betrügen, to deceive	ſaufen,[1-2] to drink (of animals)
bewegen, to induce	ſaugen, to suck
biegen, to bend	ſchallen, to resound
bieten, to offer	ſchieben, to push
fliegen, to fly	ſchießen, to shoot
fliehen, to flee	ſchließen, to shut
fließen, to flow	ſchwören, to swear
frieren, to freeze, be cold	ſieden,[1] to boil
gären, to ferment	ſprießen, to sprout
genießen, to enjoy	triefen,[1] to drip
gießen, to pour	verdrießen, to vex
heben, to lift	verlieren, to lose
kriechen, to creep	wägen, to weigh (transitive)
lügen, to tell a lie	wiegen, to weigh (intrans.)
melken, to milk	weben, to weave
riechen, to smell	ziehen,[1] to pull

(b)

dreſchen, to thresh	quellen, to gush out
erlöſchen,[2] to be extinguished	ſcheren,[4] to shear
fechten,[3] to fence, fight	ſchmelzen, to melt
flechten,[3] to plait	ſchwellen, to swell

404. Class 8 (u, a). Tragen, *to carry*.

tragen   trägt   trug   getragen   trage

backen,[5] to bake	graben, to dig
fahren, to go (by vehicle)	laden,[6] to load

[1] Imperfect and past participle: ſoff, geſoffen; ſott, geſotten; troff, getroffen; and zog gezogen. Present indicative: ſäuft.
[2] Present indicative: ſäuft, erliſcht.
[3] Present indicative: ficht, flicht.
[4] Present indicative: ſchert or ſchiert.
[5] The strong form of the imperfect is buk. In conversation, backen backt, backte, gebacken are usual.
[6] Present indicative: lädt. Laden, to invite, may form ladet.

ſchaffen,[1] to create			wachſen, to grow		
ſchlagen, to strike			waſchen, to wash		
tragen, to carry					

405. Class 9. Irregular verbs with past participle in =n or =en.

gehen	geht	ging	gegangen	gehe	to go
ſein	iſt	war	geweſen	ſei	to be
ſtehen	ſteht	ſtand	geſtanden	ſtehe	to stand
tun[2]	tut	tat	getan	tue	to do
werden	wird	wurde	geworden	werde	to become

406. Class 10. Irregular verbs with past participle in =t.

brennen	brennt	brannte	gebrannt	brenne	to burn
kennen[3]	kennt	kannte	gekannt	kenne	to know
nennen	nennt	nannte	genannt	nenne	to name
rennen	rennt	rannte	gerannt	renne	to run
ſenden	ſendet	ſandte	geſandt	ſende	to send
wenden[4]	wendet	wandte	gewandt	wende	to turn
bringen	bringt	brachte	gebracht	bringe	to bring
denken	denkt	dachte	gedacht	denke	to think
haben	hat	hatte	gehabt	habe	to have
wiſſen[3]	weiß	wußte	gewußt	wiſſe	to know

407. Class 11. Modal auxiliary verbs.

dürfen	darf	durfte	gedurft	—	to be allowed
können	kann	konnte	gekonnt	—	to be able
mögen	mag	mochte	gemocht	—	to like
müſſen	muß	mußte	gemußt	—	to be obliged
ſollen	ſoll	ſollte	geſollt	—	to owe
wollen	will	wollte	gewollt	wolle	to wish

---

[1] Present indicative: ſchafft; imperfect: ſchuf.

[2] Present: ich tue, du tuſt, er tut, wir tun, ihr tut, ſie tun.   Imperfect: ich tat, du tatſt, er tat, wir taten, ihr tatet, ſie taten.

[3] Kennen means *to be acquainted with*, and wiſſen means *to be aware of*: Ich kenne ihn, *I know him*; Ich weiß das, *I know that*. *To know by heart* is auswendig wiſſen.

Present of wiſſen: ich weiß, du weißt, er weiß, wir wiſſen, ihr wißt, ſie wiſſen.

[4] Wendete and gewendet are also used for the imperfect and past participle.

408. Alphabetical list. The following is a list of the most important strong and irregular verbs, arranged alphabetically. The second and third columns give the third person singular of the present indicative and the first person singular of the imperfect indicative respectively. Less common alternative forms are given in brackets. The vowel of the imperfect subjunctive is not given unless it is irregular.

For the contraction of the second person singular of the present indicative of verbs ending in a sibilant (e.g., beißen, bu beißeſt or bu beißt), see paragraph **372.**

Compounds formed from these verbs are generally not given, unless they are conjugated differently.

Verbs conjugated with ſein are marked *.

Infinitive	Present Indicative	Imperfect	Past Participle	Imperative	Imp. Subj.	Meaning
¹backen	bäckt	buk¹	gebacken	backe		to bake
*befehlen	befiehlt	befahl	befohlen	befiehl¹	ö (ä)	to command
beginnen	beginnt	begann	begonnen	beginne		to begin
beißen	beißt	biß	gebiſſen	beiße		to bite
bergen	birgt	barg	geborgen	birg		to save
*berſten	birſt	barſt (o)	geborſten	birſt	ö (ä)	to burst
betrügen	betrügt	betrog	betrogen	betrüge		to deceive
*bewegen³	bewegt	bewog	bewogen	bewege		to induce
biegen	biegt	bog	gebogen	biege		to bend
bieten	bietet	bot	geboten	biete		to offer
binden	bindet	band	gebunden	binde		to bind
bitten	bittet	bat	gebeten	bitte		to ask, request

¹ In conversation, backen, backt, backte, gebacken are usual.
² (Ver)fehlen, to miss, is weak.   ³ Bewegen, to move, is weak.

Infinitive	Present Indicative	Imperfect	Past Participle	Imperative	Imp. Subj.	Meaning
blaſen	bläſt	blies	geblaſen	blaſe		to blow
*bleiben	bleibſt	blieb	geblieben	bleibe		to remain
braten	brät	briet	gebraten	brate		to roast
brechen	bricht	brach	gebrochen	brich		to break
brennen	brennt	brannte	gebrannt	brenne	brennte	to burn
bringen	bringt	brachte	gebracht	bringe		to bring
denken	denkt	dachte	gedacht	denke		to think
dreſchen	driſcht	droſch (α)	gedroſchen	driſch		to thresh
*dringen	dringt	drang	gedrungen	dringe		to press
dürfen	darf	durfte	gedurft	—		to be allowed
1empfehlen	empfiehlt	empfahl	empfohlen	empfiehl	ö	to recommend
2erbleichen	erbleicht	erblich	erblichen	erbleiche		to fade away
3erlöſchen	erliſcht	erloſch	erloſchen	erliſche		to be extinguished
4erſchrecken	erſchrickt	erſchrak	erſchrocken	erſchrick		to be frightened
eſſen	ißt	aß	gegeſſen	iß		to eat
5*fahren	fährt	fuhr	gefahren	fahre		to go (by vehicle)
*fallen	fällt	fiel	gefallen	falle		to fall
fangen	fängt	fing	gefangen	fange		to catch
fechten	ficht	focht	gefochten	ficht		to fence, fight
finden	findet	fand	gefunden	finde		to find
flechten	flicht	flocht	geflochten	flicht		to plait
*fliegen	fliegt	flog	geflogen	fliege		to fly

1 (Ver)fehlen, to miss, is weak.

2 Bleichen, to bleach, and erbleichen, to turn pale, are weak.

3 Erlöſchen, to extinguish, is weak.

4 Erſchrecken, to frighten, is weak.

5 Willfahren, to comply with, is weak.

Infinitive	Present Indicative	Imperfect	Past Participle	Imperative	Imp. Subj.	Meaning
*fliehen	fliehst	floh	geflohen	fliehe		to flee
*fließen	fließt	floß	geflossen	fließe		to flow
fressen	frißt	fraß	gefressen	friß		to eat (of animals)
*frieren	friert	fror	gefroren	friere		to freeze, be cold
*¹gären	gärt	gor	gegoren	gäre		to ferment
*²gebären	gebiert	gebar	geboren	gebier		to bear (children)
geben	gibt	gab	gegeben	gib		to give
*gedeihen	gedeiht	gedieh	gediehen	gedeihe		to thrive
*gehen	geht	ging	gegangen	gehe		to go
*gelingen	gelingt	gelang	gelungen	es gelinge	ö (ü)	to succeed (impers.)
gelten	gilt	galt	gegolten	gilt		to be worth
*genesen	genest	genas	genesen	genese		to recover (health)
genießen	genießt	genoß	genossen	genieße		to enjoy
*geschehen	geschieht	geschah	geschehen	es geschehe		to happen (impers.)
gewinnen	gewinnt	gewann	gewonnen	gewinne	ö (ü)	to win
gießen	gießt	goß	gegossen	gieße		to pour
gleichen	gleicht	glich	geglichen	gleiche		to resemble
³gleiten	gleitet	glitt	geglitten	gleite		to glide
graben	gräbt	grub	gegraben	grabe		to dig
greifen	greift	griff	gegriffen	greife		to grasp
⁴haben	hat	hatte	gehabt	habe		to have
halten	hält	hielt	gehalten	halte		to hold
hangen	hängt	hing	gehangen	hange		to hang

1 Gären, *to ferment* figuratively with excitement, is weak.
2 Gebärt is usual in conversation, instead of gebiert.
3 Begleiten, *to accompany*, is weak.
4 Handhaben, *to handle*, is weak.

Infinitive	Present Indicative	Imperfect	Past Participle	Imperative	Imp. Subj.	Meaning
hauen	haut	hieb	gehauen	haue		to hew
heben	hebt	hob	gehoben	hebe		to lift
heißen	heißt	hieß	geheißen	heiße		to be called
helfen	hilft	half	geholfen	hilf	ü (ä)	to help
kennen	kennt	kannte	gekannt	kenne	kennte	to know
klingen	klingt	klang	geklungen	klinge		to sound
kneifen	kneift	kniff	gekniffen	kneife		to pinch
*kommen	kommt	kam	gekommen	komme		to come
können	kann	konnte	gekonnt	—		to be able
*kriechen	kriecht	kroch	gekrochen	krieche		to creep
¹laden	lädt	lud	geladen	lade		to load
²lassen	läßt	ließ	gelassen	laß		to let
*laufen	läuft	lief	gelaufen	laufe		to run
³leiden	leidet	litt	gelitten	leide		to suffer
leihen	leiht	lieh	geliehen	leihe		to lend
lesen	liest	las	gelesen	lies		to read
liegen	liegt	lag	gelegen	liege		to lie
lügen	lügt	log	gelogen	lüge		to tell a lie
meiden	meidet	mied	gemieden	meide		to shun
⁴melken	melkt	molk	gemolken	melke		to milk
messen	mißt	maß	gemessen	miß		to measure
mögen	mag	mochte	gemocht	—		to like
müssen	muß	mußte	gemußt	—		to be obliged

¹ Laden, to invite, may form ladet in the present.   ² Veranlassen, to cause, is weak.

³ Bemitleiden, to pity, is weak.   ⁴ Sometimes milkt in the present and milk in the imperative.

Infinitive	Present Indicative	Imperfect	Past Participle	Imperative	Imp. Subj.	Meaning
nehmen	nimmt	nahm	genommen	nimm		to take
nennen	nennt	nannte	genannt	nenne	nennte	to name
pfeifen	pfeift	pfiff	gepfiffen	pfeife		to whistle
preisen	preist	pries	gepriesen	preise		to praise
*quellen	quillt	quoll	gequollen	quill		to gush out
raten	rät	riet	geraten	rate		to advise
reiben	reibt	rieb	gerieben	reibe		to rub
reißen	reißt	riß	gerissen	reiße		to tear
*¹reiten	reitet	ritt	geritten	reite		to ride
*rennen	rennt	rannte	gerannt	renne	rennte	to run
riechen	riecht	roch	gerochen	rieche		to smell
²ringen	ringt	rang	gerungen	ringe		to wrestle
*rinnen	rinnt	rann	geronnen	rinne	ö (ä)	to flow
rufen	ruft	rief	gerufen	rufe		to call
saufen	säuft	soff	gesoffen	saufe		to drink (of animals)
saugen	saugt	sog	gesogen	sauge		to suck
³schaffen	schafft	schuf	geschaffen	schaffe		to create
*⁴schallen	schallt	scholl	geschollen	schalle		to resound
*scheiden	scheidet	schied	geschieden	scheide		to part
scheinen	scheint	schien	geschienen	scheine		to shine, seem
schelten	schilt	schalt	gescholten	schilt	ö (ä)	to scold
⁵scheren	schert	schor	geschoren	schere		to shear

¹ Bereiten, *to prepare*, is weak.   ² Umringen, *to surround*, is weak.
³ Weak with other meanings (*e.g.*, *to be occupied*, or verschaffen, *to procure*).   ⁴ Also weak.
⁵ Sometimes schiert in the present and schier in the imperative. Bescheren, *to give as a present*, is weak.

Infinitive	Present Indicative	Imperfect	Past Participle	Imperative	Imp. Subj.	Meaning
ſchieben	ſchiebt	ſchob	geſchoben	ſchiebe		to push
ſchießen	ſchießt	ſchoß	geſchoſſen	ſchieße		to shoot
ſchlafen	ſchläft	ſchlief	geſchlafen	ſchlafe		to sleep
¹ſchlagen	ſchlägt	ſchlug	geſchlagen	ſchlage		to strike
*ſchleichen	ſchleicht	ſchlich	geſchlichen	ſchleiche		to creep
ſchleifen	ſchleift	ſchliff	geſchliffen	ſchleife		to grind
ſchließen	ſchließt	ſchloß	geſchloſſen	ſchließe		to shut
ſchlingen	ſchlingt	ſchlang	geſchlungen	ſchlinge		to sling
ſchmeißen	ſchmeißt	ſchmiß	geſchmiſſen	ſchmeiße		to fling
*²ſchmelzen	ſchmilzt	ſchmolz	geſchmolzen	ſchmilz		to melt
ſchneiden	ſchneidet	ſchnitt	geſchnitten	ſchneide		to cut
ſchreiben	ſchreibt	ſchrieb	geſchrieben	ſchreibe		to write
ſchreien	ſchreit	ſchrie	geſchrie(e)n	ſchreie		to scream
*ſchreiten	ſchreitet	ſchritt	geſchritten	ſchreite		to stride
ſchweigen	ſchweigt	ſchwieg	geſchwiegen	ſchweige		to be silent
*²ſchwellen	ſchwillt	ſchwoll	geſchwollen	ſchwill		to swell
*ſchwimmen	ſchwimmt	ſchwamm	geſchwommen	ſchwimme	ö (ä)	to swim
ſchwingen	ſchwingt	ſchwang	geſchwungen	ſchwinge	ü (ö)	to swing
ſchwören	ſchwört	ſchwor (n)	geſchworen	ſchwöre		to swear
³ſehen	ſieht	ſah	geſehen	ſieh		to see
*ſein	iſt	war	geweſen	ſei		to be
⁴ſenden	ſendet	ſandte	geſandt	ſende	ſendete	to send
⁴ſieden	ſiedet	ſott	geſotten	ſiede		to boil
ſingen	ſingt	ſang	geſungen	ſinge		to sing
ſinken	ſinkt	ſank	geſunken	ſinke		to sink
*ſinnen	ſinnt	ſann	geſonnen	ſinne	ö (ü)	to meditate

¹ Rathſchlagen, *to deliberate*, and veranſchlagen, *to estimate*, are weak,   ² Weak when transitive.
³ Imperative also ſiehe.   ⁴ Sieden, *to boil* figuratively with rage, is weak.

Infinitive	Present Indicative	Imperfect	Past Participle	Imperative	Imp. Subj.	Meaning
sitzen	sitzt	saß	gesessen	sitze		to sit
sollen	soll	sollte	gesollt	—	sollte	to owe
speien	speit	spie	gespie(e)n	speie		to spit
spinnen	spinnt	spann	gesponnen	spinne	ö (ä)	to spin
sprechen	spricht	sprach	gesprochen	sprich		to speak
*sprießen	sprießt	sproß	gesprossen	sprieße		to sprout
*springen	springt	sprang	gesprungen	springe		to jump
stechen	sticht	stach	gestochen	stich		to sting
stehen	steht	stand	gestanden	stehe		to stand
¹stehlen	stiehlt	stahl	gestohlen	stiehl	ä (ü)	to steal
*steigen	steigt	stieg	gestiegen	steige		to **mount**
*sterben	stirbt	starb	gestorben	stirb	ü	to die
stoßen	stößt	stieß	gestoßen	stoße		to push
streichen	streicht	strich	gestrichen	streiche		to stroke
streiten	streitet	stritt	gestritten	streite		to quarrel
²tragen	trägt	trug	getragen	trage		to carry
treffen	trifft	traf	getroffen	triff		to meet, hit
treiben	treibt	trieb	getrieben	treibe		to drive
*³treten	tritt	trat	getreten	tritt		to step
³triefen	trieft	troff	getroffen	triefe		to drip
⁴trinken	trinkt	trank	getrunken	trinke		to drink
⁴tun	tut	tat	getan	tue		to do

¹ *To steal* in the sense of *to move quietly* is i. stehlen.
² Beauftragen, *to commission*, is weak.
³ Also triefte, getrieft in imperfect and past participle.
⁴ Present participle: tuend. For the present and imperfect in full, see paragraph 405.

Infinitive	Present Indicative	Imperfect	Past Participle	Imperative	Imp. Subj.	Meaning
verbergen	verbirgt	verbarg	verborgen	verbirg		to hide
*verderben	verbirbt	verdarb	verborben	verbirb	ü	to spoil
verdrießen	verdrießt	verdroß	verdrossen	verdrieße		to vex
vergessen	vergißt	vergaß	vergessen	vergiß		to forget
verlieren	verliert	verlor	verloren	verliere		to lose
verschwinden	verschwindet	verschwand	verschwunden	verschwinde		to disappear
verzeihen	verzeiht	verzieh	verziehen	verzeihe		to pardon
*wachsen	wächst	wuchs	gewachsen	wachse		to grow
wägen	wägt	wog	gewogen	wäge		to weigh (fig.)
waschen	wäscht	wusch	gewaschen	wasche		to wash
weben	webt	wob	gewoben	webe		to weave
*weichen	weicht	wich	gewichen	weiche		to give way
weisen	weist	wies	gewiesen	weise		to show
³wenden	wendet	wandte	gewandt	wende	wendete	to turn
werben	wirbt	warb	geworben	wirb	ü	to woo
*werden	wird	wurde (ward)	geworden	werde		to become
werfen	wirft	warf	geworfen	wirf	ü	to throw
wiegen	wiegt	wog	gewogen	wiege		to weigh
winden	windet	wand	gewunden	winde		to wind
wissen	weiß	wußte	gewußt	wisse		to know
wollen	will	wollte	gewollt	wolle	wollte	to wish
ziehen	zieht	zog	gezogen	ziehe		to pull, move
zwingen	zwingt	zwang	gezwungen	zwinge		to force

---

1 Generally weak when transitive. 2 Weichen, to soften, is weak.
3 Wendete and gewendet are also used for the imperfect and past participle.

STRONG AND WEAK VERBS

409. Strong and weak verbs. Some strong verbs become weak when they are transitive or have a different meaning, and others have weak compounds. The following are the most important:

Strong	*Weak*
bewegen, to induce	bewegen, to move
erbleichen, to fade away	bleichen, to bleach
	erbleichen, to turn pale
erschrecken, to be frightened	erschrecken, to frighten
fahren, to travel	willfahren, to comply with
befehlen, to command	(ver)fehlen, to miss
empfehlen, to recommend	
gleiten, to glide	begleiten, to accompany
haben (irreg.), to have	handhaben, to handle
lassen, to let	veranlassen, to cause
leiden, to suffer	bemitleiden, to pity
(er)löschen, to be extinguished	löschen, to extinguish
reiten, to ride	bereiten, to prepare
ringen, to wrestle	umringen, to surround
schaffen, to create	(ver)schaffen, to procure
scheren, to shear	bescheren, to give as a present
schlagen, to strike	ratschlagen, to deliberate
	veranschlagen, to estimate
schmelzen, to melt (intrans.)	schmelzen, to melt, smelt (trans.)
schwellen, to swell (intrans.)	schwellen, to swell (trans.)
tragen, to carry	beauftragen, to commission
verderben, to spoil (intrans.)	verderben,[1] to spoil (trans.)
weichen, to give way	weichen, to soften

Er glitt aus dem Zimmer	He glided out of the room
Er begleitete mich	He accompanied me
Der Schnee ist geschmolzen	The snow has melted
Die Sonne hat den Schnee geschmelzt	The sun has melted the snow

[1] The strong form is often used transitively.

CAUSATIVE VERBS

410. Causative or factitive verbs.

(a) Some verbs are related to each other like the English verbs *to fall* and *to fell*, *to lie* and *to lay*, the strong verb being intransitive and the weak transitive. The following are the most important:

Strong (Intransitive)	*Weak* (Transitive)
dringen, to force one's way	drängen, to push, press
ertrinken, to be drowned	ertränken, to drown
fahren, to travel	führen, to lead
fallen, to fall	fällen, to fell
hangen,[1] to hang	hängen, to hang
liegen, to lie	legen, to lay, put
	f. legen, to lie down
(er)schallen,[2] to resound	schellen, to ring
schwimmen, to swim	schwemmen, to float
(ver)sinken, to sink	senken, to sink
sitzen, to sit	setzen, to set, put
	f. setzen, to sit down
springen, to spring, jump	sprengen, to burst, blow up
verschwinden, to vanish	verschwenden, to waste
Er saß auf dem Stuhl	He sat (or was sitting) on the chair
Er setzte sich auf den Stuhl	He sat down on the chair
Er lag auf seinem Bett	He lay (or was lying) on his bed
Er legte sich auf sein Bett	He lay down on his bed
Er legte sein Buch auf das Pult	He put his book on the desk

(b) All the four following verbs are transitive, though saugen and trinken may be used intransitively as in English:

saugen, to suck	säugen, to suckle
trinken, to drink	tränken, to water, give to drink to

[1] In popular speech, hängen is often used in the present tense instead of hangen.

[2] Erschallen is strong, schallen often weak.

VERBS CONJUGATED WITH Sein

411. Verbs conjugated with sein. Many German verbs are conjugated with sein. The following are the most important:

(a) Sein, *to be*; bleiben, *to remain*.

(b) Intransitive verbs denoting a change of condition:

aufwachen, to wake up	gedeihen, to thrive
einschlafen, to fall asleep	sterben, to die
erkranken, to fall ill	bersten, to burst
genesen, to recover	schmelzen, to melt
erbleichen, to fade away	schwellen, to swell
erlöschen, to be extinguished	wachsen, to grow
erschrecken, to be frightened	werden, to become

(c) The following take the dative (gelingen, glücken, and geschehen are impersonal):

gelingen }to succeed glücken }	begegnen, to meet
geschehen, to happen	folgen, to follow

(d) Intransitive verbs of movement, such as gehen, *to go*; kommen, *to come*; erscheinen, *to appear*; verschwinden, *to disappear*:

Er ist von seiner Krankheit genesen	He has recovered from his illness
Es ist ihnen gelungen, die Aufgabe zu lösen	They succeeded in solving the problem
Was ist geschehen?	What has happened?
Er ist mir gefolgt	He has followed me
Er ist ins Haus gegangen	He has gone into the house

412. Only intransitive verbs may take sein. All transitive and reflexive verbs take haben:

Der Schnee ist geschmolzen	The snow has melted
Die Sonne hat den Schnee geschmelzt	The sun has melted the snow
Er hat sich hingesetzt	He has sat down

413. Haben is occasionally used with intransitive verbs of movement when the emphasis is on the action, and not on the object reached or the result attained:

Er hat (or ift) die ganze Zeit geeilt	He hurried all the time
Er ift ins Haus geeilt	He hurried into the house

XI

VERBS (*continued*)

THE INFINITIVE

414. The gerund, or infinitive used as noun.

(a) In German the definite article is generally used with the gerund, except in proverbs. For declension and examples, see paragraph **53.**

(b) In English the gerund has the same form as the present participle; in German it has the same form as the infinitive:

Infinitive	*Gerund*	*Present Participle*
to give	giving	giving
geben	das Geben	gebend

415. The English gerund followed by an object. The German gerund does not take an object; the genitive is used instead, unless, as often happens, the gerund is replaced by an ordinary infinitive:

Das Lesen eines guten Buches ist ein Vergnügen, *or*
Ein gutes Buch zu lesen ist ein Vergnügen, *or*
Es ist ein Vergnügen, ein gutes Buch zu lesen

Reading a good book is a pleasure

416. The English gerund preceded by a preposition is translated in various ways:

(a) By a gerund or ordinary infinitive:

Er besitzt die Kunst des Redens — He has the art of speaking
Er besitzt die Kunst, deutlich zu reden — He has the art of speaking clearly
Wir hatten keine Gelegenheit zum Schreiben (or zu schreiben) — We had no chance of writing

(b) If the German construction needs a preposition, the preposition is often joined to da . . . or dar . . . and put immediately before an infinitive with zu:

Er rechnet darauf, mich zu treffen	He is counting on meeting me
Ich habe nichts dagegen, weiter zu gehen	I have no objection to going further

(c) If the English gerund is preceded by a possessive noun or adjective, a clause is used in German:

Er rechnet darauf, daß sein Bruder mich trifft	He is counting on his brother's meeting me
Ich habe nichts dagegen, daß er weiter geht	I have no objection to his going further

(d) If the gerund is used in an adverb phrase, it is translated either by a gerund preceded by a preposition or by a clause beginning with a conjunction:

Beim Lesen des Briefes lächelte er, or	On (the) reading (of) the letter he smiled
Als er den Brief las, lächelte er	On reading the letter he smiled

417. The infinitive without zu.

(a) The infinitive without zu is used after the modal auxiliary verbs and lassen [see paragraph 383].

(b) An infinitive depending on the following verbs is also used without zu: fühlen, *to feel*; hören, *to hear*; sehen, *to see*; bleiben, *to remain*; and, in some phrases, gehen and other verbs of movement.

Ich höre, sehe ihn kommen	I hear, see him coming
Er blieb stehen	He stopped (or stood still)
Ich gehe schlafen	I am going to bed
Ich bin spazieren gegangen, gefahren	I have been for a walk, a ride

(c) An infinitive without zu is also sometimes used with verbs depending on heißen, *to bid* or *order*; helfen, *to help*; lehren, *to teach*; and lernen, *to learn*:

Er hilft mir schwimmen[1]	He is helping me to swim
Er lehrt mich schwimmen[1]	He is teaching me to swim

(d) Haben is used with gut in the expression

Er hat (Sie haben usw.) gut reden, lachen usw.	It is all very well for him (you, etc.) to talk, laugh, etc.

418. The infinitive with zu.

(a) Except for the constructions mentioned in the preceding paragraph, the infinitive in German is generally used with zu. If anything else is added to the infinitive, the phrase is preceded by a comma.

Ich habe einen Brief zu schreiben	I have a letter to write
Das ist nicht leicht zu verstehen	That is not easy to understand
Er fing an zu laufen	He began to run
Er versuchte, die Tür aufzumachen	He tried to open the door

(b) In a subordinate clause, the infinitive with zu is generally put before the verb (without commas), unless it is felt that this makes the sentence too long or awkward:

Obgleich das nicht leicht zu verstehen ist	Although that is not easy to understand
Als er die Tür aufzumachen versuchte (or Als er versuchte, die Tür aufzumachen)	When he tried to open the door

(c) After sein, *to be*; bleiben, *to remain*; scheinen, *to seem*; and stehen, *to stand*, the infinitive with zu translates the English passive infinitive:

Dieses Haus ist zu verkaufen	This house is for sale (to be sold)
Der Erfolg bleibt abzuwarten	The result remains to be seen

---

[1] Or Er hilft mir beim Schwimmen; Er lehrt mich das Schwimmen.

(d) For the use of the prepositions (an)ftatt and ohne with the infinitive, see paragraph **306**.

419. The infinitive with um . . . zu.

(a) Um . . . zu is used to express a purpose. Phrases with um . . . zu are separated from the rest of the sentence by a comma:

Er fetzte fich hin, um die Zei= tung zu lefen	He sat down to read the newspaper
Um das zu tun, braucht man viel Geduld	To do that you need a great deal of patience

(b) Um . . . zu is often used instead of zu after genug, *enough*; zu, *too*; and zu viel, *too much*:

Er hat Geld genug, (um) das Gefchäft zu kaufen	He has enough money to buy the business
Er ift zu müde, (um) das Buch zu lefen	He is too tired to read the book

420. The English infinitive is not always translated by the German infinitive:

(a) The infinitive after *how*,[1] *when*, *where*, or *what* is translated by a subordinate clause:

Sagen Sie mir, wann ich kommen foll	Tell me when to come
Ich weiß nicht, was ich tun foll	I do not know what to do

(b) After many verbs, particularly fagen, *to say* or *tell*, and verbs of wishing, liking, expecting, believing, and knowing, the infinitive after an object is translated by a subordinate clause:

Ich werde ihm fagen, daß er kommen foll	I shall tell him to come
Ich will (or wünfche), daß er kommt	I want him to come
Ich erwarte, daß er kommt	I expect him to come
Ich weiß, daß es wahr ift	I know it to be true

---

[1] Wiffen zu sometimes translates *to be able to* or *to know how to:* Er weiß zu reden, zu fchweigen, *He knows how to talk, to keep silent.*

(c) An object followed by an infinitive may be used in German after verbs of request, permission, advice, compulsion, or prohibition, and, where a corresponding English construction is possible, after the verbs in paragraph **417** (b) (taking an infinitive without 3u):

Er bat mich zu kommen	He asked me to come
Er erlaubte, riet, verbot mir zu kommen	He allowed, advised, forbade me to come
Ich sah ihn kommen	I saw him come

(d) An English infinitive preceded by a word governed by a preposition cannot be translated literally: *e.g.*, *I waited for him to go* would be Ich wartete, daß (or bis) er ging (if he did go), or Ich wartete, daß er ginge (if he did not go).

He was waiting for the train to come in could be translated Er wartete auf die Ankunft des Zuges.

THE PARTICIPLES

421. Use of participles. Present and past participles may be used as nouns [paragraph **52** (c)], adjectives [paragraph **172**], or adverbs [paragraph **200**].

422. Participial phrases.

(a) Participles are used in phrases in apposition, and are generally put last in the phrase:

Die fremde Stadt durchschritt ich sorgenvoll	Thinking of the children, etc.
Der Kinder denkend, die ich ließ zu Haus	
Er hat, im Schloß verborgen, Zum Schlaf sich hingesetzt	Hidden in the castle, etc.

(b) Participles are also used in adjectival phrases before nouns, the participle being declined in the ordinary way:[1]

Eine mit einem Schloß ver= sehene Tür	A door provided with a lock

423. 3u+present participle form. The same form as the present participle (really an infinitive with =b added) has the force of the English passive infinitive. As it has passive meaning, it is used only with transitive verbs:

Ein zu lesendes Buch	A book to be read
Die zu verrichtende Arbeit	The work to be done

424. The English present participle. The present participle is not as much used in German as in English. The following constructions are used in translating it:

(a) Adverb clause of time with als, indem, or während:

Als er zum Bahnhof ging, traf er Herrn A.	Going to the station, he met Mr. A.
Indem er am Tisch saß,[2] schrieb er den Brief	Sitting at the table, he wrote the letter

(b) Adverb clause of time with als or nachdem:

Als (or nachdem) er sich hin= gesetzt hatte, fing er an zu schreiben	Having sat down, he began to write

(c) Adverb clause of reason:

Da ich wußte, daß es spät wurde, eilte ich davon	Knowing that it was getting late, I hurried away

(d) Relative clause:

Ein Mann, der eine Pfeife rauchte, saß mir gegenüber	A man smoking a pipe sat opposite to me

---

[1] This construction may make a sentence long and unwieldy, and should be used cautiously. We could say, instead, eine Tür, die mit einem Schloß versehen ist.

[2] Indem may also denote means; see paragraph **328 (b)**.

(e) Two co-ordinate clauses:

Er setzte sich hin und fing an   Sitting down, he began to
zu schreiben   write

425. After gehen and kommen, the past participle is
used instead of the English present participle:

Er kam gelaufen, geritten   He came running, riding

THE SUBJUNCTIVE MOOD

426. The subjunctive mood, in general, expresses doubt,
uncertainty, or unreality.   The following are the principal
ways in which it is used:

427. To express a wish, or (as imperative in the third
person) a command:

O König, mögest du ewig   O king, live for ever
leben

Man vergesse nicht, daß . . .   Let it not be forgotten
                    that . . .

**428. Imperfect or pluperfect subjunctive instead of
conditional.**

(a) The use of the imperfect subjunctive instead of the
conditional is the rule with the verbs dürfen, können,
mögen, müssen, and sollen,[1] and common with haben and
sein and with strong verbs.   Thus, *I should like* is ich möchte
(not ich würde mögen); *I should have,* ich hätte or ich würde
haben; *I should be,* ich wäre or ich würde sein; *I should hold,*
ich hielte or ich würde halten.

This shortened form is not generally used with regular
weak verbs, as the imperfect subjunctive has the same
form as the imperfect indicative.   Thus, *I should build* is
ich würde bauen, not ich baute.

(b) The pluperfect subjunctive is more often used with
all verbs than the conditional perfect.   Thus, *I should
have built* is ich hätte gebaut or ich würde gebaut haben;

[1] To form the conditional of wollen, the auxiliary werden is
generally used.

I should have come is id) wäre gefommen or id) würde ge=
fommen sein. Similarly in the passive, *it would have been
built* is es wäre gebaut worden or es würde gebaut worden sein.

429. To express hesitation or reserve:[1]

Id) dädjte, (es wäre möglid))	I should think (it would be possible)
Dürfte id) Sie fragen, ob . . .?	Might I ask you whether . . .?

430. Reported speech or thought.

The subjunctive is
used in noun clauses containing reported statements,
questions, or thoughts, when the situation or occurrence
suggested is in doubt or contrary to fact:

Er sagt, daß er Hilfe braudje	He says that he needs help
Er sagte, daß er Hilfe braudje	He said that he needed help
Id) fragte, ob er es wisse	I asked whether he knew it
Er wünsdjte, daß er seinen Freund gesehen hätte	He wished that he had seen his friend

431. Tense used in reported speech.

(a) The general rule in such sentences as those in the
preceding paragraph is to use in the noun clause the tense
that would have been used when the words were spoken:
if the words used are " *I need help*," " *Do you know it?*",
they are reported in the present subjunctive.[2]

(b) If, in the person and number used, the present
indicative and present subjunctive have the same form, the
imperfect subjunctive is used (as in Nos. 2 and 4 of the
following examples):

Er sagte, er sdjreibe nod)	He said he was still writing
Er sagte, sie sdjrieben nod)	He said they were still writing

---

[2] In practice, this rule is not strictly observed; the imperfect
subjunctive is often used instead of the present subjunctive.

| Er fragte, ob er das Buch ge= lesen habe | He asked whether he had read the book |
| Er fragte, ob sie das Buch gelesen hätten | He asked whether they had read the book |

432. Indicative or subjunctive.

(a) The subjunctive of reported speech or thought is less used in conversation than in the literary style, and less when the verb of the main clause is in the present than when it is in the past:

Ich fürchte, es ist schwer	I am afraid it is difficult
Ich wünsche, daß er kommt	I want him to come
Ich hoffe, er kommt heute	I hope he is coming today
Fragen Sie ihn, ob er es weiß	Ask him whether he knows it
Er befahl, daß man die Tür zuschließen sollte[1]	He ordered that the door should be shut

(b) Sometimes the indicative or subjunctive is used to suggest the probability or improbability of a statement:

| Er sagt, er ist müde | He says he is tired (and there is no reason to doubt it) |
| Er sagt, er sei müde | He says he is tired (but it may be untrue) |

(c) Similarly, the indicative or subjunctive may be needed to show that something did, or might, or did not happen:

Er freute sich, daß er seinen Freund gesehen hatte	He was glad that he had seen his friend
Er wünschte, daß er seinen Freund gesehen hätte	He wished that he had seen his friend
Ich wartete, daß er ging	I waited for him to go (if he did go)
Ich wartete, daß er ginge	I waited for him to go (if he did not go)
Er sollte alles berichten, was er sah	He was to report all that he saw (at the moment)

[1] After expressions of command, sollen is often used; it is generally in the indicative, except in the literary style.

Er sollte alles berichten, was er sähe	He was to report everything that he saw (later on, or that he might see)

433. Clauses of purpose. Damit generally takes the subjunctive in the formal style and the indicative in the conversational style:

Damit er sich nicht verletzt (formal style, verletze)	So that he shall not hurt himself
Damit er sich nicht verletzen sollte	So that he should not hurt himself
Damit er kommen kann	So that he can come
Damit er kommen konnte	So that he could come

434. Als ob and **als wenn** are generally followed by the imperfect subjunctive (though the present indicative is sometimes used, as in English, if probability is implied):

Er spricht, als ob (or als wenn) er krank wäre[1]	He speaks as if (or as though) he were ill
Er tat, als ob (or als wenn) er mich nicht gehört hätte[1]	He pretended not to have heard me

435. Clauses of condition.

(a) Wenn, meaning *if*, takes the indicative in the present and future, and the subjunctive in the past:[2]

Wenn wir krank sind, (so) bleiben wir zu Hause	If (or when) we are ill, we stay at home
Wenn wir krank waren, (so) blieben wir zu Hause	When(ever) we were ill, we stayed at home
Wenn wir krank wären, (so) würden wir zu Hause bleiben	If we were ill, we should stay at home
Wenn wir krank gewesen wären, (so) würden wir zu Hause geblieben sein, or (so) wären wir zu Hause geblieben	If we had been ill, we should have stayed at home

[1] Ob or wenn may be omitted, and the inverted order used: Er spricht, als wäre er krank, etc.

[2] Wenn, meaning *when*, takes the indicative, as it introduces no suggestion of unreality.

(b) Sollen is often used in the imperfect subjunctive:[1]

Wenn er heute abend kommen   If he should (or were to)
  sollte   come this evening

(c) The future may be used after wenn, but the English *will* must often be translated by wollen instead of by the future [see paragraph **394** (b)]:

Ich will die Stelle übersetzen,   I will translate the passage
  wenn Sie mir helfen wollen   if you will help me

(d) For the omission of wenn and the use of the inverted order, see paragraph **337** (b).

436. Further use of the subjunctive. The use of the subjunctive in noun clauses, as in paragraph **430,** is extended to other kinds of subordinate clauses, and to main clauses, to disclaim responsibility for statements made or views expressed. This kind of construction is common in newspaper reports:

Herr A. könne keinen Rat   (It was felt or stated that)
  geben, da er die Sache nicht   Mr. A. could give no ad-
  verstehe   vice, on the ground that
                      he did not understand the
                      matter

REFLEXIVE VERBS

437. Reflexive verbs. The present tense of reflexive verbs (with the accusative and dative) is given in paragraph **71.** The reflexive pronoun takes the same position as any personal pronoun used as the direct or indirect object:

Present: ich irre mich (nicht), I am (not) mistaken
      irre ich mich (nicht)? am I (not) mistaken?

Future: ich werde mich (nicht) irren, I shall (not) be mistaken
      werde ich mich (nicht) irren? shall I (not) be mistaken?

Perfect: ich habe mich (nicht) geirrt, I have (not) been mis-
      taken
      habe ich mich (nicht) geirrt? have I (not) been
      mistaken?

Reflexive verbs are always conjugated with haben.

---

[1] Occasionally the imperfect subjunctive of werden is used after wenn (wenn er kommen würde), but this is not to be recommended.

438. Common reflexive verbs. Verbs are used reflexively more in German than in English. Some of those that take certain prepositions are given in paragraphs **289-305**. The following verbs are also common; those in section **(a)** take the accusative, and those in section **(b)** the dative:

(a)

ſ. befinden, to be (found)
ſ. bemühen, to take pains
ſ. beſinnen, to reflect
ſ. betragen, to behave
ſ. erholen, to recover (health)
ſ. erkälten, to catch cold

ſ. fragen (ob), to wonder (whether)
ſ. ſetzen, to sit down
(ſ.) ſtürzen, to rush
ſ. unterhalten, to converse
ſ. verirren, to lose one's way

Wir bemühten uns umſonſt — All our trouble was in vain
Ich habe mich erkältet[1] — I have caught a cold

(b)

ſ. vornehmen, to purpose, design
ſ. zuziehen, to incur

ſ. einbilden ⎫ to imagine
ſ. vorſtellen ⎭

Ich nahm mir zu viel vor — I undertook too much
Ich zog mir ſeinen Verdruß zu — I incurred his displeasure

439. With some verbs, which may be used reflexively or non-reflexively, the reflexive pronoun is generally not translated into English:

ändern, to change
ankleiden, to dress
fühlen, to feel
lehnen, to lean

raſieren, to shave
treffen, to meet
trennen, to part, separate
waſchen, to wash

Er lehnte ſich an die Wand — He leaned against the wall
Er lehnte den Stock an die Wand — He leaned the stick against the wall
Ich fühlte mich zum Schweigen verpflichtet — I felt obliged to say nothing
Ich fühlte die Hitze — I felt the heat
Wir trennten uns um ſechs Uhr — We parted at six o'clock
Wir trennten die Streiter — We parted the quarrellers

---

[1] Ich bin erkältet, *I have a cold.*

IMPERSONAL VERBS

440. Impersonal verbs. When a verb is used impersonally, it is in the third person singular, with the subject es: es regnet, *it is raining*; es wundert mich, *I am surprised*. Verbs used impersonally can be classified as follows:

(a) Those describing natural phenomena:

es blitzt, there is lightning
es donnert, it is thundering
es dunkelt, it is getting dark
es friert (zu), it is freezing

es hagelt, it is hailing
es regnet, it is raining
es schneit, it is snowing
es taut (auf), it is thawing

(b) Those taking the accusative:

es ärgert mich,[1] I am annoyed
es dürstet mich,[2] I am thirsty
es ekelt mich,[1] I am disgusted
es freut mich,[1] I am glad
es friert mich,[3] I am cold

es hungert mich,[2] I am hungry
es verdrießt mich, I am vexed
es wundert mich,[1] I am surprised

(c) Those taking the dative:

es fällt mir ein, it occurs to me
es tut mir leid, I am sorry
es tut mir weh, it hurts me
es tut mir wohl, it does me good

es gefällt mir, I like it
es gelingt mir ⎱ I succeed
es glückt mir ⎰
es ist mir warm (kalt), I am warm (cold)

The verbs in paragraphs (b) and (c), and similar verbs, may invert and drop the es: Mir ist gelungen (or Es ist mir gelungen), den See zu durchschwimmen, *I succeeded in swimming across the lake.*

Many may also be used as ordinary verbs, with a noun or pronoun as subject: Die Sache ärgerte mich sehr, *The matter annoyed me very much*; Das Haus gefällt mir, *I like the house.*

---

[1] Also ich freue mich, *I am glad*, etc.
[2] Also ich habe Durst, Hunger.
[3] Also ich friere, *I am cold.*

(d) Those used reflexively:

es empfiehlt sich, it is advisable

es ergibt sich, it follows

es fragt sich, it is questionable

es handelt sich um, it is a question of

es läßt sich [see paragraph **395 (b)**]

es lohnt sich, it is worth while

es schickt sich, it is proper

es versteht sich, it is a matter of course

(e) Many verbs may be used in the passive to denote an action without specifying the subject. The es is translated by *there,* and is omitted if the inverted or transposed order is used:

Es wurde den ganzen Abend gelacht, gesungen usw., or Den ganzen Abend wurde gelacht, gesungen usw.

There was laughing, singing, etc., going on all evening

Man konnte hören, daß den ganzen Abend gelacht, gesungen wurde

You could hear that there was laughing, etc.

USE OF TENSES

441. The present.

(a) In German, as in English, the present tense is often used when referring to the near future:

Ich komme am Dienstag wieder

I am (or shall be) coming back on Tuesday

(b) The historical present is often used, especially in poetry, to make a narrative more vivid. It is generally better to translate it by the past:

Jetzt, da er dem Sänger ins Auge sah,
Da ergreift ihn der Worte Bedeuten

Now, looking into the singer's eyes, he suddenly realised what the words meant

(c) To describe what has been, and still is, taking place, the German present is used for the English perfect. This construction is often used with seit, *since,* and schon, *already.*

The imperfect is used in the same way for the English pluperfect to describe what had been, and still was, taking place:

Er ift ſchon drei Tage (or ſeit drei Tagen) hier	He has been here three days (and is still here)
Er war ſchon drei Tage (or ſeit drei Tagen) hier	He had been here three days (and was still here)
Er ift immer unwohl, ſeit(dem) der Unfall geſchehen ift	He has been unwell ever since the accident happened
Es ift das erſte Mal, daß ich Deutſchland beſuche	It is the first time that I have visited Germany (being still there)
Seit wann ſind Sie hier?	How long have you been here?

442. The future is sometimes used (especially with wohl), as in English, to denote probability:

Sie werden das (wohl) ſchon gehört haben	You will probably have heard that already

443. The imperfect and past definite.

(a) As there are no continuous tenses in German, there is no distinction in form between the imperfect and the past definite. Thus the imperfect, ich baute, means *I built* or *I was building*, just as the present, ich baue, means *I build* or *I am building*.

(b) An habitual action in the past may be expressed by the imperfect of pflegen, *to be accustomed to*, or by the imperfect without pflegen: *I used to build* may be ich pflegte zu bauen or ich baute.

444. The imperfect and perfect.

(a) In general, the imperfect tense is used in German to narrate connected events in the past in relation to each other (as in the English *I saw him and spoke to him*); and the perfect is used to describe past actions from the point of view of their effect on the present (as in the English *I have seen him and spoken to him*).

(b) Sometimes the Germans (except in South Germany) use the imperfect for the English perfect: Waren Sie ſchon in Berlin? *Have you ever been in Berlin?* On the other hand, it is more common for the German perfect to be used for the English past definite, especially in conversation, and in South Germany. All the verbs in the following passage would be better translated by the past definite: *I finished my homeward pilgrimage*, etc.:

Ich habe die Wallfahrt nach meiner Heimat mit aller An-dacht eines Pilgrims vollendet, und manche unerwarteten Gefühle haben mich ergriffen. An der großen Linde . . . ließ ich halten, stieg aus, und ließ den Postillon fortfahren.

CASES AFTER VERBS

445. The nominative is used as the complement of in-transitive verbs, such as sein, *to be*; scheinen, *to seem*; bleiben, *to remain*; werden, *to become*; heißen,[1] *to be called*:

Es war ein kalter Tag	It was a cold day
Er hieß Karl der Große	He was called Charlemagne
Er blieb ein Schuft	He remained a rascal

446. The accusative.

(a) The direct object of a transitive verb is in the accusative:

Ich schreibe einen Brief	I am writing a letter
Ich sah den Unfall	I saw the accident

(b) Verbs of naming take a second accusative, as complement of the direct object:

Er nannte (or hieß) ihn einen Schuft	He called him a rascal

If this construction is made passive, the two accusatives become nominatives:

Er wurde ein Schuft genannt (or geheißen)	He was called a rascal

(c) Lehren, *to teach*, takes two accusatives:

Er lehrt mich Geschichte[2]	He teaches me history

[1] Heißen, *to call*, takes the accusative; see next paragraph.
[2] It is more common to use unterrichten: Er unterrichtet mich in der Geschichte.

(d) Bitten and fragen take an accusative of person, but neither takes anything but a neuter pronoun as accusative of thing.

Nur das möchte ich Sie bitten	I should only like to ask you (to do) that (for me)
Nur das möchte ich Sie fragen	I should only like to ask you that (one question)

To ask, meaning *to beg* or *to request,* is bitten; *to ask,* meaning *to inquire,* is fragen:

Ich bat ihn um seine Antwort	I asked him for his answer
Ich bat ihn, es zu tun	I asked him to do it
Ich fragte ihn nach seinem Alter	I asked him his age

To ask a question is eine Frage richten or stellen:

Er richtete (or stellte) eine Frage an den Jungen	He asked the boy a question

447. Verbs governing the genitive.

(a) The following reflexive verbs govern the genitive:

s. bedienen, to make use of	s. erbarmen, to have mercy on
s. befleißigen, to apply oneself to	s. erfreuen, to enjoy, rejoice in
s. bemächtigen, to take possession of	s. erinnern, to remember
s. enthalten, to abstain from	s. rühmen, to boast of
s. entledigen, to get rid of	s. schämen, to be ashamed of
s. entwöhnen, to disaccustom oneself to	

Das Heer bemächtigte sich der Stadt	The army took possession of the town
Er rühmte sich seiner Heldentaten	He boasted of his exploits

In three of these verbs, the following constructions are optional: s. entwöhnen von; s. erbarmen über (accusative); s. erinnern an (accusative).

(b) The following verbs may govern the genitive or accusative:

bedürfen, to need	erwähnen, to mention
entbehren, to do without	gedenken,[1] to remember, think of
entraten, to dispense with	

Er bedarf keiner (or keine) Hilfe — He needs no help

Er gedenkt seiner Freunde — He remembers his friends

(c) A few verbs take the accusative of person and genitive of thing; the following are the most important:

anklagen }　to accuse of	berauben, to rob of
beschuldigen }	versichern, to assure of

Er klagte ihn des Verbrechens an (or Er beschuldigte ihn des Verbrechens) — He accused him of the crime

448. Verbs governing the dative.

(a) The following verbs govern the dative:

ähneln }　to resemble	gehorchen, to obey
gleichen }	gelingen, to succeed
begegnen, to meet	gratulieren, to congratulate
bekommen[2] }　to suit	helfen, to help
passen }	lauschen, to listen to
danken, to thank	nahen, to approach
dienen, to serve	nützen, to be of use
drohen, to threaten	schaden, to injure
fluchen, to curse	schmeicheln, to flatter
folgen, to follow	trotzen, to defy
gefallen, to please	vertrauen,[3] to trust

---

[1] Gedenken takes the accusative in the sense of remembering something against someone: Das will ich dir gedenken, *I will make you pay for that.*

[2] Bekommen, *to get,* takes the accusative.

[3] *To entrust,* with dative of person and accusative of thing, is generally anvertrauen.

Of these verbs, begegnen, folgen, and gelingen are conjugated with fein, and gelingen is impersonal:

Er dankte mir	He thanked me
Ich bin ihm gefolgt	I have followed him
Es ist mir gelungen	I have succeeded
Er hilft mir oft	He often helps me

(b) The following verbs, among many others, take a
dative of person and accusative of thing:

beantworten, to answer	leihen, to lend
befehlen,[1] to command	neiden, to envy
bezahlen,[2] to pay	raten, to advise
bringen, to bring, take	schicken, to send
erlauben, to allow	verbieten, to forbid
geben, to give	verdanken, to owe
glauben,[3] to believe	vergeben, to forgive
kosten,[4] to cost	

Beantworten Sie mir die Frage	Answer me the question
Ich schickte ihm das Paket	I sent him the parcel
Ich glaube (es) Ihnen	I believe you (in what you say)

(c) With a few verbs—*e.g.*, entreißen, *to snatch*; nehmen,
to take; rauben, *to rob*; stehlen, *to steal*—the dative is used
for the English *from*:[5]

Er nahm, entriß, stahl ihm das Buch	He took, snatched, stole the book from him

Nehmen corresponds to the French *prendre à, to take from*.
To take a thing to a person is translated by bringen or tragen:

Er brachte ihm das Buch	He took the book to him

[1] *To command* in the sense of commanding an army or fleet is
befehligen or über (ein Heer, eine Flotte) befehlen.

[2] Ich bezahle ihn; ich bezahle das Geld; ich bezahle ihm das Geld.

[3] A noun object of glauben is put into the dative: Ich glaube seinen
Worten.

[4] Kosten may also take the accusative of person and of thing.

[5] Verbergen, *to hide*, also takes this construction, but verbergen vor
+ dative is often used, especially when referring to material objects:
Er verbarg mir seinen Schmerz; Er verbarg sich vor seinen Feinden.

(d) Many verbs take a dative through being compounded with **ent=**, **wider=**, or a preposition taking the dative; *e.g.*, **zu**:

Er entging der Strafe	He escaped punishment
Er widersprach mir	He contradicted me
Er rief ihm die Antwort zu	He shouted the answer to him
Er wohnte dem Fußballspiel bei	He attended the football match

449. The dative of interest or advantage. The dative is often used in German to show interest or advantage:

(a) For its use with reflexive and impersonal verbs, see paragraphs **438** (b) and **440** (c).

(b) It is often used with transitive or intransitive verbs where the English use the nominative or accusative:

Es macht dem Jungen Angst	It frightens the boy
Das will ich dir gedenken	I will pay you out for that
Er ließ es seinen Kindern zugute kommen	He let his children have the benefit of it
Es blieb mir (or Mir blieb) eine Mark übrig	I had a shilling left

(c) It is often used where the English use the possessive noun or adjective:

Er fiel seinen Feinden in die Hände	He fell into his enemies' hands
Ich wasche mir die Hände	I wash my hands

(d) The ethic dative is a construction in which a personal pronoun is used to indicate less direct interest or concern:

Laß schlafen mir den Alten	Let the old man sleep, I tell you

THE PASSIVE

450. Conjugation of passive verbs. See paragraph **351.**

451. Werden and fein.

(a) The passive is formed by the auxiliary verb werden and the past participle of the verb to be conjugated:

Ich trage den Rock	I wear the coat (active)
Der Rock wird von mir ge= tragen	The coat is worn by me (passive)

(b) A passive verb denotes an action, past, present, or future. If the auxiliary fein is used instead of werden, a state, not an action, is expressed, and the past participle has the force of an adjective:

Die Tür wird um zehn Uhr geschlossen	The door is shut (*i.e.*, the shutting takes place) at ten o'clock
Die Tür ist jetzt geschlossen	The door is now (already) shut

(c) As in the active, a continuous tense may be needed in English:

Die Tür wird jetzt geschlossen	The door is now being shut

(d) Geboren, *born*, generally takes fein when referring to the living, and werden when referring to the dead:

Ich bin 1922 geboren	I was born in 1922
Luther wurde 1483 geboren	Luther was born in 1483

452. Avoiding the passive. The passive need not always be avoided in translating into German, but it is less used in German than in English. The following constructions may sometimes be used:

(a) The sentence may be made active, especially if the German verb is intransitive [see also next paragraph]. Thus, *His character has been affected by his occupation* might be translated Sein Beruf hat auf seinen Charakter gewirkt.

(b) When a more definite subject is not available, man may be used with the verb in the active:

Man beschloß also, zu Fuß　So it was decided to walk
　heimzukehren　　　　　　　home

(c) Sometimes the verb is used reflexively:

Der Saal füllte sich schnell　　The hall was quickly filled

(d) Sometimes lassen is used (1) reflexively (Es läßt sich nicht leugnen, *It cannot be denied*) or (2) non-reflexively (Er läßt ein Haus bauen, *He is having a house built*); see paragraphs **395** (b) and (c).

(e) For the translation of the passive infinitive after sein, bleiben, scheinen, and stehen (*e.g., This house is to be sold*), see paragraph **418** (c).

453. The dative.

(a) When the form of a sentence is changed to make an active verb passive, the direct object becomes the subject.

(b) An intransitive verb has no direct object, and therefore cannot be made passive in this way. This means that with some verbs—*e.g.,* danken, *to thank*; helfen, *to help*; widersprechen, *to contradict* (which in German are intransitive, as they take the dative case)—a different construction must be used if they are made passive.

(c) If an intransitive verb is made passive, an impersonal construction must be used:

Es wurde mir gedankt, ge-　I was thanked, helped, con-
　holfen, widersprochen　　　tradicted

If the inverted or transposed order is used, es is omitted:

Mir wurde gedankt usw.　　I was thanked, etc.

(d) With verbs that take a direct and an indirect object, only the direct object in the active may become the subject in the passive; the words in the dative do not change:

Er zeigte mir den Brief　　He showed me the letter
Der Brief wurde mir von ihm　The letter was shown me by
　gezeigt　　　　　　　　　him

The English construction that changes a word from the dative to the nominative (*He showed me the letter—I was shown the letter by him*) is impossible in German.

(e) The simplest way of translating the English passive with these verbs is generally to make them active, using **man** if no agent is stated:

Er zeigte mir den Brief	He showed me the letter (or I was shown the letter by him)
Man zeigte mir den Brief	I was shown the letter
Er folgte mir	He followed me (or I was followed by him)
Man folgte mir	I was followed

PREFIXES

454. Prefixes.

(a) German verbs are often compounded with prefixes. These are of three kinds: (1) always inseparable; (2) always separable; (3) sometimes separable and sometimes inseparable.

(b) When the prefix is inseparable, the stress falls on the stem of the verb: **be'ginnen**; when it is separable, the accent falls on the prefix: **'ankommen**.

455. Inseparable prefixes.

(a) Seven prefixes are always inseparable: **be-, ge-, er-, ver-, zer-, emp-,** and **ent-**.

(b) The only irregularity in verbs taking these prefixes is that they do not add **ge-** in the past participle:

beginnen	begann	begonnen	to begin
gefallen	gefiel	gefallen	to please
erreichen	erreichte	erreicht	to reach
verbieten	verbot	verboten	to forbid
zerbrechen	zerbrach	zerbrochen	to smash
empfehlen	empfahl	empfohlen	to recommend
entgehen	entging	entgangen	to escape

456. Separable prefixes.

(a) Most separable prefixes are prepositions or adverbs. There are many of them; among the commonest are **an=, auf=, aus=, bei=, ein=, her=, hin=, mit=, nach=, vor=,** and **zu=.**

(b) These verbs are conjugated as follows:

ankommen	kam an	angekommen	to arrive
hersagen	sagte her	hergesagt	to recite
mitteilen	teilte mit	mitgeteilt	to inform
zumachen	machte zu	zugemacht	to shut

457. Position of the prefix.

(a) It will be seen from the previous section that the **ge=** of the past participle comes between the prefix and the stem. When the infinitive with **zu** is used, the **zu** is put in the same way between the prefix and the stem:

Er gedenkt, morgen anzu= kommen	He expects to arrive to- morrow
Er ist noch nicht angekommen	He has not yet arrived

(b) When a simple tense of the verb is used, the prefix is separated from the verb and put last in the sentence, unless the sentence is in the transposed order, when the prefix is not separated:

Er nahm den Vorschlag an	He accepted the proposal
Nimmt er den Vorschlag an, or Wenn er den Vorschlag annimmt	If he accepts the proposal

458. Verbs formed with nouns or adjectives.

(a) Some verbs, formed with nouns or adjectives, are conjugated similarly, the noun or adjective being treated as a separable prefix; the noun is spelt with a small letter:

achtgeben, to pay attention	festhalten, to hold fast
kundtun, to make known	freisprechen, to acquit
preisgeben, to abandon	hochachten, to esteem
stattfinden, to take place	loswerden, to get rid of
teilnehmen, to take part	wahrnehmen, to perceive

Die Versammlung findet heute abend statt	The meeting takes place this evening

Der Angeklagte wurde freige=   The accused was acquitted
sprochen

(b) Some verbs formed from or compounded with nouns
or adjectives are weak verbs conjugated like **bauen**, the
prefix being inseparable:

frühstücken, to have breakfast	ratschlagen, to deliberate
handhaben, to handle	rechtfertigen, to justify
langweilen, to bore, weary	wetteifern, to vie, compete

Ich habe noch nicht gefrüh=   I have not had breakfast yet
stückt

Er versuchte, seine Tat zu   He tried to justify his
rechtfertigen   action

(c) There are certain verbal phrases in common use,
made up of preposition, noun, and verb, the preposition
and noun generally being written as one word, and the
verb taking its ordinary conjugation. **Zumute sein** is impersonal:

imstande sein, to be able	zustande kommen, to come
instand setzen, to enable, re-pair	about
vonstatten gehen, to progress	zumute sein, to feel
zugrunde gehen, to be ruined	zuliebe tun, to do in order to please
zugute kommen lassen, to give someone the benefit of something	

Er ließ es seinen Kindern zu=   He let his children have the
gute kommen   benefit of it

Dem Mann war nicht wohl   The man did not feel happy
zumute   (or easy in his mind)

Er tat es seinem Vater zuliebe   He did it to please his father

459. Double prefixes. If the first part of a double prefix
is inseparable, the whole is inseparable. Otherwise, any
separable part is treated as separable:

Er beaufsichtigt die Arbeit	He is supervising the work
Ich erkenne seine Fähigkeit an	I recognise his ability
Ich gehe eben hinaus	I am just going out

460. Doubtful prefixes : durdᷓ=, ḥinter=, miß=, über=, um=, unter=, voll=, wider=, and wieder=. These prefixes are sometimes used separably and sometimes inseparably.

Generally, when they are used separably the verb has its full literal meaning, and when they are used inseparably a less literal meaning. The stress varies accordingly:

'wiederḥolen	ḥolte wieder	wiedergeḥolt	to fetch or bring back
wieder'ḥolen	wiederḥolte	wiederḥolt	to repeat

461. Wieder= is always separable, except in **wiederḥolen**, *to repeat*.

462. Ḥinter=, voll=, and wider= are nearly always inseparable.

(a) Although **ḥinter=** is occasionally separable according to the dictionaries, it is in practice inseparable. The following are the commonest compounds:

ḥinterbringen, to inform, denounce	ḥinterlaſſen, to leave behind (on death)
ḥintergeḥen, to deceive	ḥintertreiben, to frustrate
ḥinterlegen, to deposit	ḥinterzieḥen, to embezzle

(b) Voll= is always inseparable, except when used quite literally:

Jdᷓ ḥabe den Koffer voll= gepackt	I have packed the suit-case full
Er ḥat ſeinen Auftrag voll= zogen	He has carried out his commission

The commonest compounds of **voll=** (inseparable) are:

vollbringen, to accomplish	vollfüḥren ⎫
vollenden, to finish	vollſtrecken ⎬ to carry out
	vollzieḥen ⎭

(c) Of the compounds of **wider=**, widerḥallen, *to echo*, and widerſpiegeln, *to reflect*, are used both separably and inseparably. The following are the commonest inseparable compounds; those marked (D) take the dative:

widerfahren (D), to befall
widerlegen, to refute
widerraten (D), to dissuade
widerrufen, to revoke
ſ. widerſetzen (D), to oppose
widerſtehen (D), to resist

widerſprechen (D), to contradict
widerſtreben (D), to conflict with
widerſtreiten (D), to contest

463. Miß= is inseparable, except sometimes in the past participle and occasionally in the infinitive with zu. Miß=ſtimmen, *to put out of humour*, takes mißzuſtimmen and mißgeſtimmt. Mißdeuten, *to misinterpret*, takes zu miß=deuten or mißzudeuten, and mißdeutet or mißgedeutet. Usually the ordinary inseparable construction is correct. The following are the commonest compounds:

mißachten, to despise
mißbrauchen, to misuse
mißdeuten, to misinterpret
mißfallen, to displease
mißglücken[1] }
mißlingen[1] } to fail

mißgönnen, to grudge
mißtrauen, to mistrust
mißverſtehen, to misunderstand

The following past participles are used as adjectives:

mißgeartet, degenerate
mißgebildet, malformed

mißgelaunt, out of humour
mißgeſtaltet, misshapen

464. Durch= and um= are used a good deal both separably and inseparably. The principal compounds of **durch=** are as follows:

(a) Always separable:

durchfallen, to fall through, fail
durchführen, to carry through
durchhelfen, to help through
durchlaſſen, to let through

durchmachen, to go through (*e.g.*, a war)
durchnehmen, to go through (*e.g.*, a book)
durchprügeln, to thrash soundly

[1] Impersonal.

(b) Always inseparable:

durchlöchern, to perforate	durchschweifen, to roam through
durchkreuzen, to cross	
durchnässen, to wet through	durchstöbern, to ransack

(c) Separable or inseparable with a difference of meaning:

	Separable	*Inseparable*
durchblicken } durchschauen }	to look through (lit.)	to see through
durchbohren	to pierce (literally)	to pierce (figuratively)
durchbrechen	to break . . . through	to break through . . .
durchsetzen	to carry through	to mix, intersperse

Er brach den Stock durch	He broke the stick through
Sie durchbrachen die Linie	They broke through the line

(d) Some verbs of movement are intransitive when the prefix is separable, and transitive when it is inseparable:

durchdringen, to penetrate	durchlaufen, to run through
durchfahren } durchreisen } to travel through	durchwandern, to walk or wander through

Er ist durch die Stadt (durch)=gereist	He has travelled through the town
Er hat das ganze Land durch=reist	He has travelled through the whole country

465. Um.

(a) Um= is used separably with three meanings:

(i) *Afresh* or *over again*:

Er hat den Aufsatz umge=arbeitet	He has remodelled the essay
Sie müssen in Leipzig um=steigen	You must change at Leipzig

(ii) *Down:*

Der Wagen wurde umge=   The car was overturned
worfen

Die Fahne wurde umgerissen   The flag was torn down

(iii) *In a reverse sense:*

Er kehrte auf demselben Wege   He retraced his steps
um

So wurde die ganze Sache   In that way the whole affair
umgewandelt   was transformed

(b) Umbringen, *to kill,* and umkommen, *to perish,* are
separable. See also bringen and kommen with the preposition um, paragraph **302** (a).

(c) When used inseparably, **um=** generally means *round*
or *roundabout,* either literally or figuratively. The following are common inseparable verbs:

umarmen, to embrace   ummauern, to wall in
umgarnen, to ensnare   umschließen, to enclose, sur-
umgeben, to surround   round

(d) Some compounds are used separably and inseparably
with different meanings:

	Separable	*Inseparable*
umfassen	to reset	to include, com-prise
umgehen (mit)	to associate (with)	to avoid
umgraben	to dig up	to dig round
umschreiben	to rewrite	to paraphrase
umstellen	to transpose	to surround

466. Über= and unter=.

(a) **Über=** and **unter=** are used in many compounds, and
are generally inseparable unless used in a literal, physical
sense:

Er setzte mich (über den Fluß)   He took me across (the river)
herüber or hinüber

Er übersetzte die Aufgabe   He translated the exercise

Er hat seinen Namen (unter die Schrift) untergeschrieben	He has signed his name (under the writing)
Er hat den Brief unterschrieben	He has signed the letter

(b) The following compounds of **unter=** are separable:

unterbringen, to shelter, dispose of	unterkommen, to find lodgings or employment
untergehen, to sink, perish	unterordnen, to subordinate

(c) There are many inseparable compounds of **über=** and **unter=**. The following are typical examples:

übergeben, to deliver, surrender	überwiegen, to predominate
überfallen, to attack suddenly	unterbrechen, to interrupt
	unterliegen, to succumb
überreden, to persuade	unternehmen, to undertake
	unterwerfen, to subjugate

AGREEMENT OF SUBJECT AND VERB

467. Agreement of subject and verb.

(a) A collective noun, such as die Menge, *mass, crowd, quantity*, or die Anzahl, *number*, generally takes the verb in the singular; but if it is thought of as a number of separate persons or things, the verb may be in the plural:

Eine Anzahl Leute stand (or standen) vor dem Rathaus	A number of people were standing in front of the town-hall

(b) Ein paar, and other expressions meaning *a few*, take a plural verb.

(c) Two or more nouns may be treated as one subject, with the verb in the singular, if they are thought of as a single unit; otherwise, the verb is in the plural:

Salz und Brot macht die Wangen rot	Salt and bread make the cheeks red
Potsdam und Brandenburg liegen nicht weit von Berlin	Potsdam and Brandenburg are not far from Berlin

(d) Two uninflected adjectives (*e.g.*, jung und alt) are sometimes used together with a singular verb; see paragraph **152**.

(e) If two pronouns of different persons are used with the same verb, the verb agrees with the first person before the second, and with the second person before the third; but where the verb has a different form for each of the two persons, it is generally better in German, as in English, to recast the sentence; thus *Either you or I must go* might be translated Einer von uns muß gehen.

SUMMARY OF WORD-ORDER

468. Word-order. Questions of word-order are dealt with under the various parts of speech concerned. The most important points are summarised in the following paragraphs.

469. Normal order. In the normal order the sentence begins with the subject (sometimes preceded by a co-ordinating conjunction), followed by the finite verb. In a compound tense the past participle, or infinitive, or past participle+infinitive, comes at the end:

Und ich habe es oft gesehen	And I have often seen it
Ich werde die Aufgabe schreiben	I shall write the exercise
Ich werde die Aufgabe geschrieben haben	I shall have written the exercise

470. Inverted order. In the inverted order, the subject comes immediately after the finite verb,[1] the past participle and infinitive still being last but one and last. This order is used:

(a) In commands:

Kommen Sie bald wieder!	Come again soon

(b) In questions:

Kommen Sie bald wieder?	Are you coming again soon?

[1] The subject is occasionally put later in the sentence; see, for example, paragraph 135 (d).

(c) Sometimes to emphasise a statement as a whole:

Bar das eine Freude!　　　What a delight that was!

(d) Sometimes instead of using wenn, *if*:

Hätte ich das gewußt, (so wäre　If I had known that, (I
ich nicht gekommen)　　　should not have come)

(e) In a main clause preceded by a clause subordinate
to it:[1]

(Da ich zu früh angekommen　(As I had arrived too early,)
war,) mußte ich warten　　　I had to wait

(f) In a main clause, when any words, other than the
subject or a conjunction, come before the finite verb:[2]

Am nächsten Abend kam er　The next evening he came
wieder　　　　　　　　　again
Das kann ich leicht verstehen　I can easily understand that

(g) For the use of the inverted order with doch meaning
for, see paragraph **214** (e).

471. Transposed order. In the transposed order the
verb comes last, the auxiliary, if any, being last of all.[3]
The transposed order is used in subordinate clauses [for
exceptions—omission of daß, and inversion instead of
wenn—see paragraphs **327** (b) and **337** (b)]:

(Ich weiß nicht,) ob er heute　(I do not know) whether he
gekommen ist　　　　　　　has come today. (*Noun
　　　　　　　　　　　　clause*)
(Hier ist mein Freund,) der　(Here is my friend) who has
eben angekommen ist[4]　　just arrived. (*Adjective
　　　　　　　　　　　　clause*)

---

[1] For an exception concerning adverb clauses of concession,
see paragraph **319** (c).

[2] For exceptions concerning adverbs, see paragraph **241** (b) and (c).

[3] For exceptions in such constructions as weil ich habe schreiben
müssen, see paragraph **387**.

[4] It would be correct, and common in conversation, to use der
as a demonstrative pronoun, and say Hier ist mein Freund; der ist
eben angekommen, *Here is my friend; he has just arrived* (two main
clauses).

| (Ich mußte warten,) da ich zu früh angekommen war | (I had to wait,) as I had arrived too early. (*Adverb clause*) |

472. Two objects, direct and indirect. Two nouns, dative first. Two personal pronouns, accusative first. Noun and pronoun, pronoun first. Two different kinds of pronouns, personal pronoun first:

Er gab dem Reisenden die Fahrkarte	He gave the traveller the ticket
Er gab sie ihm	He gave it to him
Er gab sie dem Reisenden	He gave it to the traveller
Er gab ihm das	He gave him that

473. Adverbs. For the position of adverbs (including nicht) and adverb phrases, see paragraphs **239-241**.

474. Change of position for emphasis. The rules for word-order are often disregarded in poetry for the sake of metre, and occasionally in prose for emphasis; thus the words allwöchentlich and und starken Willen are emphasised in the following passages by Keller and Frenssen respectively.

Er haßte vielmehr die Leute beinahe, weil sie die einzigen waren, bei welchen er einige bare Pfennige herausklauben mußte allwöchentlich.

Das Leben ist lang genug, etwas aus sich zu machen, wenn einer Zutrauen hat und starken Willen.

APPENDIX

SUGGESTIONS FOR REVISION

The following scheme of lessons is suggested as a means of revising the most important points of elementary grammar during the School year, twelve lessons being given for the first term, ten for the second, and eight for the third. Every lesson contains some revision of verbs, and every third lesson is devoted entirely to verbs. The numbers refer to paragraphs.

FIRST TERM

Revision 1.

(a) Word-order: **239, 240, 241, 319, 469-472.**

(b) Verbs: gehen, sein, stehen, tun, werden.   **405, 408.**

Revision 2.

(a) Punctuation: **6, 60, 61, 173, 241 (c), 242, 244 (c), 306, 318, 418 (a).**

(b) Verbs: senden, wenden, bringen, denken, haben, wissen. **406, 408.**

Revision 3.

(a) Verbs: regular weak and strong verbs, and slight irregularities. **348, 349, 365, 368-379.**

(b) Verbs: brennen, kennen, nennen, rennen.   **406, 408.**

Revision 4.

(a) Nouns: strong declension, class **1.   23.**

(b) Verbs: essen, fressen, geben, messen, treten.   **397 (a), 408.**

Revision 5.

(a) Nouns: strong declension, class 2. 24.

(b) Verbs : vergeſſen, geſchehen, leſen, ſehen. 397 (a) and (b), 408.

Revision 6.

(a) Verbs: the passive voice. 351, 450-453.

(b) Verbs: bitten, geneſen, liegen, ſitzen. 397 (c), 408.

Revision 7.

(a) Nouns: strong declension, class 3. 25.

(b) Verbs: brechen, erſchrecken, gelten, helfen, nehmen. 398 (a), 408.

Revision 8.

(a) Nouns: weak declension. 26.

(b) Verbs: ſprechen, ſterben, treffen, verbergen, verderben. 398 (a), 408

Revision 9.

(a) Verbs: verbs conjugated with ſein. 350, 411, 412.

(b) Verbs: werfen, befehlen, empfehlen, gebären, ſtehlen. 398 (a) and (b), 408.

Revision 10.

(a) Personal pronouns. 62-64, 66-68.

(b) Verbs: beginnen, gewinnen, kommen, ſchwimmen, ſinnen. 398 (c), 408.

Revision 11.

(a) Relative pronouns. 74-84.

(b) Verbs: binden, dringen, finden, gelingen, ſingen. 399, 408.

Revision 12.

(a) Verbs: modal auxiliary verbs. **352, 380-387.**

(b) Verbs: dürfen, können, mögen, müssen, sollen, wollen. **407, 408.**

SECOND TERM

Revision 13.

(a) Demonstrative pronouns. **86-94.**

(b) Verbs: sinken, springen, trinken, verschwinden, zwingen. **399, 408.**

Revision 14.

(a) Interrogative pronouns and adjectives. **102-113.**

(b) Verbs: beißen, erbleichen, gleichen, gleiten, greifen. **400, 408.**

Revision 15.

(a) Verbs: modal auxiliary verbs and lassen. **389-395.**

(b) Verbs: leiden, pfeifen, reißen, reiten, schleichen. **400, 408.**

Revision 16.

(a) Declension of adjectives. **142-150.**

(b) Verbs: schneiden, schreiten, streichen, streiten, weichen. **400, 408.**

Revision 17.

(a) Comparison of adjectives. **155-167.**

(b) Verbs: bleiben, leihen, reiben, scheiden, scheinen. **401, 408.**

Revision 18.

(a) Verbs: the infinitive. **417-420.**

(b) Verbs: schreiben, schreien, schweigen, steigen, treiben. **401, 408.**

Revision 19.

   (a) Numbers and dates. **174, 185, 191, 194.**

   (b) Verbs: blaſen, braten, fallen, fangen, halten. **402, 408.**

Revision 20.

   (a) Expressions of time. **190, 192, 193.**

   (b) Verbs: hangen, hauen, heißen, laſſen, laufen. **402, 408.**

Revision 21.

   (a) Verbs: gerunds and participles. **414-416, 421-424.**

   (b) Verbs: raten, rufen, ſchlafen, ſtoßen. **402, 408.**

Revision 22.

   (a) Adverbs and negatives. **212, 220, 236, 238.**

   (b) Verbs: betrügen, lügen, bewegen, heben, weben. **403 (a), 408.**

THIRD TERM

Revision 23.

   (a) Prepositions with the accusative. **247-255.**

   (b) Verbs: biegen, bieten, fliegen, fliehen, fließen. **403 (a), 408.**

Revision 24.

   (a) Verbs: the subjunctive. **426-436.**

   (b) Verbs: frieren, genießen, gießen, kriechen, riechen. **403 (a), 408.**

Revision 25.

   (a) Prepositions with the dative. **256-268.**

   (b) Verbs: ſaufen, ſaugen, ſchallen, ſchieben, ſchwören. **403 (a), 408.**

Revision 26.

(a) Prepositions with the accusative or dative. **270-286.**

(b) Verbs: ſchießen, ſchließen, ſprießen, triefen. **403 (a), 408.**

Revision 27.

(a) Verbs taking the dative. **448, 449.**

(b) Verbs: verdrießen, verlieren, wägen, wiegen, ziehen. **403 (a), 408.**

Revision 28.

(a) Subordinating conjunctions. **317 (a), 319 (a)** and **(b), 320 (d)** and **(e), 321, 323, 327 (b), 330, 333, 337 (b).**

(b) Verbs: erlöſchen, fechten, quellen, ſchmelzen, ſchwellen. **403 (b), 408.**

Revision 29.

(a) The articles. **14-20.**

(b) Verbs: backen, fahren, graben, laden, ſchaffen. **404, 408.**

Revision 30.

(a) Verbs: prefixes. **455-460.**

(b) Verbs: ſchlagen, tragen, wachſen, waſchen. **404, 408.**

INDEX

The numbers refer to paragraphs